S Meeting the Saviour

The glory of Jesus in the Gospel of John

Published by
The Bible Reading Fellowship
First Floor, Elsfield Hall
15–17 Elsfield Way, Oxford OX2 8FG
Website: www.brf.org.uk

ISBN-10: 1 84101 497 4
ISBN-13: 978 1 84101 497 5
First published 2007
10 9 8 7 6 5 4 3 2 1 0

Acknowledgments
Unless otherwise stated, scripture quotations are taken from the Holy Bible, New
International Version, copyright © 1973, 1978, 1984, 1995 by International Bible
Society, and are used by permission of Hodder & Stoughton Publishers, a division
of Hodder Headline Ltd. All rights reserved. 'NIV' is a registered trademark of
International Bible Society. UK trademark number 1448790.

Extract from *The New Testament in Modern English*, Revised Edition, translated by
J.B. Phillips. Copyright © 1958, 1960, 1972 by J.B. Phillips

Graham Kendrick, Extract from 'Arise, Shine' by Graham Kendrick. Thankyou
Music/Adm. by worshiptogether.com songs excl. UK & Europe, adm. by
kingswaysongs.com tym@kingsway.co.uk Used by permission.

The Nicene Creed as it appears in *Common Worship: Services and Prayers for the
Church of England* (Church House Publishing, 2000) is copyright © The English
Language Liturgical Consultation and is reproduced by permission of the
publisher.

A catalogue record for this book is available from the British Library

Printed in Singapore by Craft Print International Ltd

Meeting the Saviour

The glory of Jesus in the Gospel of John

Derek Tidball

In memory of my mother, Joan,
who went to meet the Saviour, Christmas 2006.

Preface

This book was originally conceived as a book of short meditations on the figure of Jesus Christ as he is portrayed in the Gospel of John. The meditations were written as an aid to daily or occasional devotion rather than as a complete commentary or academic study of John. The result is 26 portraits of Jesus through which his glory shines.

In line with this, there are passages in the Gospel that have been passed over. No doubt, more portraits could have been exhibited. For example, I have not included Jesus' encounter with the woman accused of adultery (7:53—8:11), the text of which was not found in the earliest manuscripts. We could well view it as a wonderful picture of Jesus displaying his glory as the victim's champion. Here he champions the cause of the vulnerable, the case for integrity, the availability of mercy and the possibility of restoring broken lives. Once you have finished this book, perhaps you might look at the sections omitted and work out for yourself how the glory of Jesus is displayed in them as well.

Had the economics of publishing permitted, I would have loved to have interwoven these meditations with some of the great works of art that have been painted through the centuries, depicting Jesus in his various guises. To read about Jesus as the sacrificial lamb (1:29) and then to meditate in prayer on the theme with the aid of Francisco de Zurbaran's *The Bound Lamb* or to consider Jesus as the good shepherd (10:1–21) alongside a picture of the marvellous late third- or early fourth-century marble on that theme, which is in the Vatican City Museum, could bring a depth to some people's devotion that would otherwise elude them. It has not been possible to incorporate those classic works of art in this volume, but perhaps you can find them in publications like Gabriele Finaldi's *The Image of Christ: The catalogue of the exhibition Seeing Salvation* (Yale University Press, 2000), or trace them on the Internet for yourself.

I have used the NIV Inclusive edition throughout.

I wish to express my gratitude to Andrew Stobart for working through this manuscript for me, improving its English and challenging my thinking, resulting in greater clarity. I also wish to thank Naomi Starkey and the team at BRF for the wonderful work they did as the manuscript progressed. I, of course, take responsibility for the flaws and inadequacies that remain.

The introduction sets the scene and I would encourage you not to skip over it. The first section, about the majestic Prologue of the Gospel, is longer than the others but after these introductory chapters the book settles down to an even rhythm.

May this little book help you to see in new ways the glory of him who was 'full of grace and truth' (1:14)

Derek Tidball
London School of Theology

And the glory of the Lord will be revealed,
and all people will see it together.
ISAIAH 40:5

Arise, shine, for your light has come,
and the glory of the Lord rises upon you.
ISAIAH 60:1

.

We have seen his glory, the glory of the One and Only, who came
from the Father, full of grace and truth.
JOHN 1:14

We believe in one Lord, Jesus Christ,
the only Son of God,
eternally begotten of the Father,
God from God, Light from Light,
true God from true God,
begotten not made,
of one Being with the Father,
through whom all things were made.
For us and our salvation he came down from heaven,
was incarnate of the Holy Spirit and the Virgin Mary
and was made man.
For our sake he was crucified under Pontius Pilate;
he suffered death and was buried.
On the third day he rose again,
in accordance with the Scriptures;
he ascended into heaven
and is seated at the right hand of the Father.
He will come again in glory to judge the living and the dead,
and his kingdom will have no end.
THE NICENE CREED

Contents

The glory of Jesus according to John

On several occasions when the media have conducted one of those competitions to find out who has been the most influential person in history, they have excluded the figure of Jesus of Nazareth from the start. It seems that they know he is without equal. No one is in the same league as he is, whether judged by his teaching, his life, his death or his impact. But just what was it about him that made him so special? One of the answers to that question—the answer that the writer of John's Gospel would give—is that what made him special was his 'glory'. Let me explain.

The majestic opening words of John's Gospel reach a climax with the words, 'The Word became flesh and made his dwelling among us. We have seen his glory, the glory of the One and Only, who came from the Father, full of grace and truth' (1:14). John's testimony is that as he and his friends watched, listened and shared in the life of the one they knew to be Jesus from Nazareth, the son of Mary and the carpenter Joseph, they saw 'glory' in him and radiating from him. His life pulsated with glory.

Matthew, Mark and Luke write about Jesus disclosing his glory only when they record his 'transfiguration', the occasion on which his appearance changed, becoming radiant, to reveal his true nature. For them, the glory of Jesus mostly lay hidden, to be revealed in the future at the time of his coming again. But John's recollection of Jesus was that his glory was evident in his life on earth and manifest time and again in what he said and did. His life was, as it were, one prolonged transfiguration. Consequently, 'glory' becomes one of the big words of John's Gospel, along with 'light', 'life' and 'truth'.

What is 'glory'? Originally, in Greek, the word meant 'an opinion', but meanings change and grow. 'Opinion' came to be associated with 'a high opinion' or 'a good reputation', which in turn grew to mean someone worthy of honour, esteem, even worship. The Bible uses the word like this to speak of the honour that is directed to God. To worship him is to glorify him. But it also uses 'glory' to speak of the amazing power, magnificent beauty and majestic splendour that shine out from him.

Glory belongs supremely and uniquely to God. Moses and Miriam asked, 'Who among the gods is like you, O Lord? Who is like you—majestic in holiness, awesome in glory, working wonders?' (Exodus 15:11). David declared, 'Yours, O Lord, is the greatness and the power and the glory and the majesty and the splendour, for everything in heaven and on earth is yours' (1 Chronicles 29:11). Israel repeatedly celebrated God as 'the King of glory' (Psalm 24:10). God is glorious.

God gave the world a glimpse of his glory in various ways and on many occasions. His glory was his signature that could be traced in creation itself. It was seen in momentous events—as he manifested his divine power in the deliverance of the children of Israel from oppression in Egypt, and as, in thunder, lightning and cloud, the law was given on Mount Sinai. It was equally seen in the more ordinary but no less spectacular provision of daily food, as manna was deposited in the desert. The glory of the Lord filled the tabernacle and, later in Israel's story, was also to infuse and overflow from every part of Solomon's temple.

It was intended that God's glory should dwell among his people. Early in their experience, however, they became so well practised in sin that a woman named her son Ichabod, meaning 'the glory has departed from Israel' (1 Samuel 4:21). Centuries later, Ezekiel was to lament that he saw the glory depart from Jerusalem (Ezekiel 10:18). Its withdrawal triggered the catastrophe of the exile. Later, Ezekiel had another vision—a vision of a time when the glory would return, when divine displeasure would be spent and a new day would dawn, with the glory of the Lord again filling a new temple (Ezekiel 43:1–3). It was that day John believed he had seen arrive in the coming of Jesus. The glory of God was, henceforth, to be seen in the person of Jesus.

Two things are particularly surprising about John's claim. First, God's people had learned that, because of their finite humanity, they were unable to bear too much of the revelation of God's glory. Moses had asked to see God's glory but was given a mere glimpse of his back as he passed by (Exodus 33:18–33). Yet John says that in Jesus the invisible had become visible and God's glory shone plainly. Second, Isaiah, the prophet of glory, whose image of God is awesome, stated that God does not share his glory with anyone else (Isaiah 42:8, 48:11). He guards it jealously and reserves it for himself. Even more surprising, then, that John should say of Jesus, a fellow human being, that his followers saw him as the one who bore and revealed God's glory.

John presents the glory of Jesus in all the colours of a rainbow. His glory was something that he shared with God 'before the world began' (17:5, 24), and that Isaiah foresaw (12:41), but was now embodied in the incarnate Christ, living among his people (1:14; 13:32). Several miraculous acts—John calls them 'signs'—revealed his glory (2:11; 11:4). Paradoxically, though, the glory was most apparent not in the dazzling acts of power but in the disguised acts of servanthood (13:1–5), and never more so than on the cross (7:39; 12:23; 13:31). To human eyes, the crucifixion was far from glorious. It was designed to humiliate, degrade and shame. It was the most dishonourable act that human beings have ever perpetrated. Yet God triumphed through it to reveal his glory at Calvary as never before and, beyond it, the even greater glory of his risen Son.

These are the primary colours with which John paints the glory of Jesus. His glory is evident throughout the Gospel, not only when the actual word is used or the radiance patently obvious. More subtle colours, too, complete the masterpiece of Jesus' glory in John. This book surveys the primary colours, the pastel shades and the subtle hues that go to make up the portrait. We view each part of John's Gospel and ask the same question each time: 'How did people see glory in what Jesus was saying or doing here?' It is not intended to suggest that reading the Gospel through this lens exhausts its teaching. John's teaching is certainly richer and fuller than will be evident from reading it through this filter alone. Not all his ideas or doctrines will come to the surface this way—but many will.

My prayer is that we shall meet the Saviour and see again 'the glory of God in the face of Christ' (2 Corinthians 4:6), and that it will lead us to a renewed adoration of the one with whom it is all too easy to become overfamiliar. May his glory shine brightly now and grow ever more in intensity until one day we bask in the full measure of it.

—— 1 ——

The glory of the eternal word

JOHN 1:1–18

John's Gospel begins on a fortissimo. Not for him the quiet building of musical themes until they reach a climax, nor the gentle lulling of the listener, to be led seductively to a grand finale. The opening resoundin chords arouse our senses and grab our full attention from the start. Strangely, John begins with his conclusion. Immediately he confronts us with a stunning, mind-blowing, spirit-racing description of Jesus. The glory of the man of Nazareth is unmistakably the focal point, yet he is portrayed on the widest possible canvas.

John presents us with five great facts about Jesus that show him to be the matchless, peerless, unrivalled, supreme and pre-eminent one.

Jesus holds the supreme title in the universe (vv. 1–2)

Celebrities are often awarded titles. Muhammad Ali was 'the Greatest'; Don Corleone, the Godfather; Arnold Schwarzenegger, 'the Terminator'. Jesus is 'the Word'. Jews believed in a God who spoke and in doing so accomplished his purposes. The creation story is peppered with the phrase, 'And God said...'. Each time, what God commanded came into being. So the people of Israel firmly believed that 'by the word of the Lord were the heavens made, their starry host by the breath of his mouth' (Psalm 33:6). The psalmists welcomed and celebrated God's words, for they were flawless, perfect, righteous, trustworthy, true, eternal, life-directing, enlightening to the mind, sweet to the taste and nourishing to the soul. In Proverbs, his words are essentially seen as wise. Proverbs 8 pictures wisdom as a person who was with God before the creation of the world and assisted him in it. Here, then, wisdom, creation and word flow together in one stream.

For Isaiah, the word of the Lord, spoken by the prophets, always achieved what it set out to do (Isaiah 55:11). It was inconceivable that, when God spoke, he should fail to accomplish his purpose. God's word, then, was not only effective in creation but also in matters of judgment and salvation. When John designated Jesus as 'the Word', it was all this and more that was in his mind.

Greeks thought about 'the word' in a different way. To them, it stood for reason or thought: the rational basis on which the universe ran. In spite of the different nuances, however, Jew and Greek would have understood John to be saying something similar about Jesus. The mind of God was expressing itself in Jesus. God was making himself, his ways and his purposes known. God was in communication with the people he had made.

The opening verses of John's Gospel make three assertions about this Word. First, they speak of *his existence in eternity*. He was 'in the beginning'. The place to start in understanding Jesus, says John, is not with his baptism and commissioning in the River Jordan, as Mark suggests, or with his childhood in Nazareth, to which Luke alludes; nor is it sufficient to go back to his birth in Bethlehem, as both Matthew and Luke do, or even to trace his ancestry through the generations of Israel's history. To understand Jesus, we must go back to before creation, to the beginning of all things, to before the worlds were. Beyond him you cannot reach. There was never a time when he was not.

Second, the opening verses speak of *his place in the Trinity*. Twice John states that the Word was 'with God' in eternity. Here we are being given a hint of the inner life of the Trinity, which John will speak about more fully later in his Gospel. It is clear that he means more than that Jesus was merely attendant upon God—an acolyte or an angel—for he goes on, thirdly, to speak of *his nature as deity*. Not only was he 'with God' but he was God; not just partly divine but fully divine. Here is the most momentous claim to be made about Jesus. Those who shared their lives with him were in no doubt that he was a full flesh-and-blood human being. Yet, he was no mere man. He was God in a human body, fully divine as well as fully human.

Dermot McDonald captures John's meaning when he says, 'There is nothing beyond him, nothing before, nothing after, nothing more. He has no before and no after. In this "title of eternity" we have a solemn affirmation of Christ's eternal deity.'[1]

Jesus plays the supreme role in creation (vv. 3–4)

This creative Word brings something into existence out of nothing. Jesus was God's agent in bringing into being all that there is in our universe: 'Through him all things were made; without him nothing was made that has been made.' This affirmation is repeated in different but equally majestic ways in Colossians 1:15–20 and Hebrews 1:2.

It declares that there is no corner of our universe, no detail of our galaxy, no section of our wonderfully complex world that does not owe its origin to Jesus. Nothing is too big to have been created by him, and nothing too small. The highest ranges of the Himalayas, the vast reaches of the Urals, the desert stretches of the Sahara, the deep recesses of the oceans and the dense beauty of the world's forests come from his hand. The highest, widest and deepest are his creation. So too is the subatomic particle, the humble amoeba, the tiniest muscle of the body and the busy ant. The hidden things of the earth—the DNA helix, the quasars and quarks—were designed and produced by him. The far-flung stars and things we cannot readily grasp with our eyes, let alone understand with our minds, are the result of his creative genius. The sum and the parts owe their existence to him. He alone does not owe his life to another; nor did he derive it from those who have gone before. He has life in himself. All other life is dependent on him and sustained by him.

This means that Jesus is the key to the riddle of our universe. It is not fully understood by scien, nor fathomed by philosophy. Its ultimate secrets are not unlocked by a mechanistic approach or by an anthropological principle. They are unlocked by knowing Jesus.

Light is essential for life. Until God spoke, 'the earth was formless and empty [and] darkness was over the surface of the deep' (Genesis 1:2). But when the lights of heaven were switched on at his command, order was brought to the chaos, meaning filled the emptiness and life sprang out of nothingness. The world began to teem with life of every kind. No one can live without his light. The Word continues to enlighten all people, reminding them of their creatureliness before God and of their need to live in communion with him.

At the heart of our universe stands neither scientific law, nor fate, nor blind chance, but a person who can be known: the person of Jesus.

Jesus is the supreme agent of regeneration (vv. 10–13)

Men and women have perversely and consistently tried to snuff out the light that is so essential for life. They have sought to go their own way in the universe, trodden unlit paths and got lost in the fog of sin. Darkness rather than light seems now to cover the face of the earth and to be a truer description of the world in which we live. As happens in fog and darkness, we are separated from one another and alienated from our true family. We try to cope as best we can, but all our efforts testify to our lack of success. At root, our problems stem from our rejection of the light-giver who made the world. The rejection sometimes arises out of ignorance or a lack of recognition, as when we say to someone, 'I'm sorry I didn't know who you were', rather than deliberate rebellion. Either way, the result is the same: forsaking a life of dependence for one of self-centred independence causes us to be estranged from our Father and ill at ease in the world that he intended to be our home.

The Word came to make it possible for us to re-enter the family and to be received as genuine, fully accepted children of the Father once more. He has the power to bring the change about and the authority to change our status in relation to God. Just as his word was used to create the world originally, so his word is now able to recreate our lives again and reconstitute God's family.

This act of regeneration does not happen in the way in which normal human procreation takes place. It happens because the grace of God wills that it should be so. John tells us that from our side it is only necessary to recognize Jesus for who he is, receive him as Saviour and Lord, trusting that he is able to provide the means by which we can begin again, for regeneration to occur. He alone is the one through whom we can experience rebirth into the family of God.

Jesus performs the supreme wonder of incarnation (v. 14)

The Word is genuinely able to bridge the gulf between the God of eternity and his fallen human family because 'the Word became flesh'. John underlines the point with a series of echoes between verses 1, 10 and 14. In verse 1, the Word 'was'; in verse 14, the Word 'became'. In verse 1, the word 'was with God'; in verse 10, the Word 'was in the world.' In verse 1, the Word 'was God'; in verse 14, 'the Word became flesh'. In verse 1, we deal with infinity and speak of an eternal beginning; in verse 14 we deal with history and speak of an event in time.

John's words speak to us of *the humility of his humanity*. In becoming a human being, the incarnate Word entered into a new condition, not experienced by him before. What an act of divine condescension: 'Our God, contracted to a span, incomprehensibly made man', in John Wesley's memorable words! 'Flesh' seems to stress the frailty and vulnerability to which the incarnate Son was exposed. What an amazing risk God took when, as Father Neville Figgis has graphically written, 'the God who roared, who could order armies and empires around like pawns on a chess board, this God emerged in Palestine as a baby who could not eat solid food or control his bladder, who depended on a teenage couple for shelter, food and love'.[2] But the folly of God is wiser than the best of human wisdom.

This act of immense humility was to have ongoing consequences, since, in Bruce Milne's words, 'the act of self-humbling on the part of God is irreversible—he is eternally Emmanuel, God with us'.[3]

John's words equally speak of *the reality of his humanity*. In saying that Jesus 'made his dwelling among us', John emphasizes that Jesus came to reside, to be watched, tested and examined. Unlike the mythical deities of Rome, he did not continue to live in ethereal luxury, only occasionally popping into the realm that belonged to humans. Nor did he shoot down to earth as if he were some celestial politician arriving at the scene of a tragedy for a brief photo opportunity. He came to stay. Those who lived and worked with him were, then, in a good position to testify to the reality of his humanity. He was no spirit, temporarily clothed in a human body while actually escaping the real-life pressures and temptations to which ordinary beings were subject. He was one of us.

John chooses his words carefully. In saying that Jesus 'dwelt among us', he uses the language of the tabernacle in the wilderness. For the children of Israel, fresh out of Egypt, that was God's home on earth. Now, says John, the home of God could be found in Jesus—the man from Nazareth.

Jesus accomplishes the supreme act of revelation (vv. 14–18)

The fifth sphere in which Jesus is unrivalled is the sphere of revelation. No one has revealed God, and no one can reveal him, more fully than the Word. If we ask how we can know what God is like, the Christian has only one answer: God is Christ-like. All that we need to know of God, we find in Jesus. In him the invisible God has become visible, the infinite God has been expressed in the finite, the unknown has been made known and the mystery has been revealed. Jesus is the prism through whom the glory of God shines into our world.

Not content with the bald statement, however, John adds a few pointers to the kind of God Jesus revealed him to be. 'Grace and truth,' he writes, 'came through Jesus Christ.' Through Jesus, the grace of pardon, forgiveness, restoration and new life can be received. In Jesus, the truth of God can be found, trusted and followed. We need look no further.

John shows us one who was supreme as Lord of eternity, master of creativity, saviour of humanity, like us in identity yet the revealer of divinity. In him was glory, 'the glory of the One and Only'. What should be the impact of this on us? To adapt Bruce Milne's words, we should realize that 'if Jesus Christ shows us the nature of God, we are called to worship him without cessation, obey him without hesitation, love him without reservation, serve him without qualification and follow him without renunciation'.[4]

Questions

1. J.B. Phillips wrote a famous book called *Your God Is Too Small*. In the light of John 1, is your Jesus 'too small'?

2. Of all the claims made here about Jesus, which matters most to you, and why?

—— 2 ——

The glory of the sacrificial lamb

Have you ever played 'spot the celebrity'? Some years ago, while on holiday in London, we learned that a prominent national leader's memorial service was to be held that morning at Westminster Abbey. With nothing better to do, my wife and I stationed ourselves outside the main doors and enjoyed watching a multitude of well-known politicians, other celebrities and several members of the royal family arrive for the event.

It must have been something like that in Galilee when John the Baptist began to preach. The crowds turned out to see and hear the latest sensation. Amazingly, he told them not to look at him, but to look elsewhere. He pointed them to his cousin, Jesus, with the startling words, 'Look, the Lamb of God, who takes away the sin of the world!' Why did he call Jesus the Lamb of God? How was the glory of God to be displayed by a lamb?

The problem of the world

Our answer must begin not with the lamb but with the problem that the lamb came to resolve, namely the problem of sin. Some time ago, the very notion of sin would have been ridiculed, but the sad and destructive events of recent years, such as major terrorist atrocities, movements of ethnic cleansing, domestic violence, corruption in business and paedophilia, mean that even the most sceptical of our media have had to rediscover the vocabulary of sin and wickedness to explain the way human beings behave.

The Bible, in fact, does not reserve the word 'sin' for heinous acts that we would all agree were wrong. It speaks of sin in many different ways, and from a number of different perspectives. In doing so, it leaves us in no doubt that sin is a problem for 'us', not just for 'them'. We are all caught in the web of sin because we are all by nature sinners. John Goldingay writes, 'Scripture has a telling range of terms for sin: to list the most common of these, sin means failure, rebellion, transgression, trespassing, turning from the right road, stain, infidelity.'[5] Within a few verses in the middle of the account of the Day of Atonement (Leviticus 16:16, 21–22), sin is variously described as spiritual pollution, emphasizing that it defiles our lives; outright rebellion, because we engage in wilful transgression; conscious wickedness, arising from the twistedness of our fallen natures; and wrongdoing, serious or trivial, deliberate or unintentional, of thought or deed, of commission or omission.

One particularly pertinent definition of sin occurs in Romans 3:23: 'for all have sinned and fall short of the glory of God'. Refusing to excuse anyone, whatever his or her religious, ethnic or cultural background, whether Jew or Gentile, Paul asserts that none of us lives up to God's intention for us as the summit of his creation. His image in us is marred and his glory dimmed. We are living under par. We are out of sync with our Creator and, consequently, we fail to reflect his holiness in the way we live, and fail to fulfil our calling to be good stewards of his world. Since we 'fall short', we need a way of making amends. Since the glory is dimmed, we need a way for the glory to be restored.

The provision of the Lord

There is nothing we can do to redeem our situation, and yet, there is something that God has done to present us with a solution. He has provided a lamb. Echoing the story of the ram that God provided for Abraham as a sacrifice to take the place of his son Isaac, told in

Genesis 22, John proclaims that God has freely provided a lamb to meet our needs. That is why he is called the lamb *of God*.

To our way of thinking, the provision of a lamb, even if he is God's lamb, may not seem to be the obvious solution to the problem. But to those steeped in the traditions of Israel, the connection would have been immediately apparent. Lambs played the decisive role on many occasions in securing atonement for sin and freedom from the threat of death and judgment. Indeed, they occur so frequently in the rituals and stories of Israel that it is difficult to decide to which particular lamb in the Old Testament John was alluding. Perhaps he was not intending to select one above others. He probably had a more fluid, composite picture in his mind. Two Old Testament references to the lamb, and one from the New Testament, especially help to explain what John meant when he described Jesus in this way.

First, there is *the Passover lamb that delivered people from death*. Exodus 12 records that when God activated his judgment against Egypt to set his people free, the lives of the Israelites themselves were potentially forfeit because of their sin. But God devised a way to ensure that the angel of death would ignore them. A lamb was to be slain, cooked and eaten and its blood painted on the Israelites' door frames as a signal to the visiting angel to exclude them as he meted out his punishment. It was important that the door posts were painted in blood; other paint would not do. Blood symbolized the life principle, so in painting blood on the door posts the Israelites were signalling that a life had been sacrificed for their sin and offered as a substitute in their place. The lamb of God was the substitute who would secure our deliverance.

Second, there is *the suffering lamb that denied itself*. Here, the incomparable words of Isaiah 53 are in mind, especially verses 4–7. Sinners are portrayed as wayward sheep that have wandered off on their own paths instead of sticking to God's. The solution is found again in a substitute—in a willing sheep that innocently, voluntarily, silently, uncomplainingly goes to the slaughter in their place. In doing so, he bears the sins of the wayward ones, removes their iniquities and endures their punishment. His voluntary death leads to their healing and forgiveness.

Third, there is *the victorious lamb that destroys sin*. This lamb, referred to in Revelation 5:5–6, is different, for here is a lamb that conquers. The image comes as a surprise. Verse 5 leads us to believe that the one who would defeat God's enemies, destroy the power of sin and unlock the future would be a lion. We can understand why such a royal and powerful beast should be necessary to conquer evil. The image fits. But suddenly we are told that the lion is, in fact, a lamb—and a lamb who quite evidently has been slain, even though he now stands triumphantly encircled by the worshippers of heaven. The imagery stresses that God's way of dealing with the strong powers that oppose him is the way of weakness, submission, folly—indeed, of the cross.

The purpose of the Christ

The lamb comes not primarily to be a teacher, philosopher or example, still less a moralizer. He comes to be a Saviour. He comes to 'take away the sin of the world'. After a carnival or other great public event, the crowds leave mountains of rubbish behind. Then along come the road sweepers and the refuse disposal people, who take it all away, leaving the streets clean and fresh as if no litter had ever been deposited there. That is what the lamb does to the sin of the world. He removes it from us, 'as far as the east is from the west' (Psalm 103:12).

He removes the guilt of sin, cleanses the stain of sin, pardons the penalty of sin, heals the hurts of sin, destroys the power of sin and restores the brokenness that sin has caused in our lives. All the sin of the world rolled into one is not too great for him to handle. It was all dealt with on his cross. To find that Christ has relieved us of the burden of sin is freedom indeed. In *Pilgrim's Progress*, John Bunyan describes Christian's experience of this relief in these words:

I saw in my Dream, that just as Christian came up with the Cross, his Burden loosed from off his shoulders, and fell from off his back, and began to tumble, and so continued to do, till it came to the mouth of the Sepulchre, where it fell in, and I saw it no more. Then was Christian glad and lightsome, and said with a merry heart, He hath given me rest by his sorrow, and life by his death. *Then he stood still awhile to look and wonder; for it was very surprising to him, that the sight of the Cross should thus ease him of his Burden.*

The proof of the claim

How can we be sure that this is no more than wishful thinking or religious imagination? The proof of the claim comes in the verses that follow, John 1:30–42. In those verses, John the Baptist says, 'I saw…'. Here is the eyewitness account of events that happened. They have not been invented. Then the Spirit says, 'I own him…', as he comes down from heaven and remains on Jesus as he is baptized. Then the disciples say, 'We affirm him…' as they begin to investigate for themselves and test out the claims made about Jesus. Since then, countless thousands of Christians have testified, and millions still can, that he is the Lamb of God who takes away their sins, and not theirs alone but the sins of all in the world who embrace him.

John invites us to 'look' at this lamb. He does not wish us to seize a fleeting glance, nor to peer with a sceptical gaze, but to gaze with faith, in wonder that God's glory was revealed in a lamb. Looking at the lamb means that we must turn towards him from our sin, trust in him with our lives and take hold of him as our Lord.

Questions

1. Is our thinking about the problems of the world radical enough? Do we trace the problems back to 'the problem of sin' or are we content to explain the world's ills more superficially?

2. Can you testify that the Lamb of God has taken away the sin and failure of your life, once and for all? Or do you lack confidence that your sin has been forgiven because Jesus Christ came to earth?

—— 3 ——

The glory of the winemaker

JOHN 2:1–11

We probably all have our favourite stories about things that have gone wrong at weddings. Those who gathered at Cana had a story to tell that tops them all. The celebrations would have begun on a Wednesday and lasted for a week. The whole extended family and village would have been invited to the non-stop party. And that was where the problem lay: to host such a popular and lengthy event was a huge responsibility—and a huge expense. The catering bill would have been immense. What if the family responsible couldn't afford it? That's probably the explanation for what happened in Cana, at the wedding where the wine ran out.

The absence of wine was the setting for Jesus' first miracle. Through it he 'revealed his glory' and because of it 'his disciples put their faith in him' (v. 11). The miracle does not have that impact on everyone. The theologian D.F. Strauss condemned it as an unnecessary miracle of luxury in a world of real need. So why did Jesus' disciples see his glory when he changed water into wine?

The miracle shows us three things about Jesus.

It hints at his costly freedom (vv. 1–5)

Jesus seems to have had a typical Jewish mother! She wanted to show off 'her boy' and let everyone know how exceptional he was at solving problems. Perhaps she had come to depend on him as the man around the house after the death of Joseph. So, when a problem arose, she knew he'd sort it out—and what a problem this one was! The rabbis said, 'Without wine there is no joy.' How could there be a wedding without wine and without joy?

When Mary suggests that he should do something about it, Jesus' reply is respectful, but distant (v. 4). Jesus spoke in this way to declare, right from the start of his public life, that he was sovereignly free to conduct his ministry as he chose, without the interference, advice or manipulation of others. Mary, in Don Carson's words, had 'borne him, nursed him, taught his baby fingers elementary skills, watched him fall over as he learned to walk… But now he had to enter into the purpose of his coming, everything, even family ties had to be subordinated to his divine mission.'[6]

His freedom was to prove costly, however, as his reply to his mother suggests. His reluctance to do anything, he explains, is due to the fact that his 'time has not yet come'. Throughout John's Gospel there are allusions to his 'time' or 'the hour' (12:23, 27; 13:1; 17:1). They make it clear that when Jesus spoke of his 'time', he was referring to his cross. It was then that his true mission would be revealed and his purpose accomplished. It was then that he would have his hour of 'glory'—a glory that was to be made known through the shame of the cross. Would his mother have been quite so keen to call her boy in to help if she had realized the full implication of what she was asking?

It demonstrates his compassionate power (vv. 5–10)

Not put off by her son's rebuff, Mary instructs the servants to get ready to do what Jesus tells them. She may not have understood it all, but she was sure that her son would want to save the happy couple from the public disgrace of running out of wine, caused probably by their equally embarrassing lack of financial resources. And Jesus obliges. He tells the servants to fill six huge water jars with water, and at his word the water is changed into choice wine.

What compassion! William Barclay remarks on how 'Jesus, the Lord of all life, the King of Glory, used his power to save a simple Galilean lad and lass from shame and humiliation'.[7] His compassion operates on a grand scale. Verse 6 tells us the size of the jars that held the water. In contemporary terms, together they would have held around 150 gallons, or 680 litres. Perhaps Jesus was ensuring not only a great end to the wedding feast but that the couple would have a good cellar—or a good investment—for years to come.

Here is not only compassion at work, but power too. Archbishop William Temple quipped that 'the modest water saw its God and blushed'. The water drawn fresh from the well, unquestionably nothing but H_2O, was transformed into top-quality wine. This act stands as a symbol for all the times when Jesus has subsequently transformed people's emptiness into fullness, their insipid lives into exciting adventures, and their failures into fruitfulness.

It reveals his persuasive glory (v. 11)

Still, however, we have not penetrated the reason why the disciples thought they saw the glory of God in this act and came to believe in Jesus. Was it just that they were dazzled by the spectacle, or was there something more? John calls it a 'miraculous sign'. Jesus was no magician, doing conjuring tricks. Nor was he one of the many wonder-workers in the ancient world, displaying fraudulent powers. His miracles were signs that pointed to deeper realities, namely to God at work rescuing his world and to who Jesus himself truly was. The reason the disciples came to believe in him was that, when they saw him work this miracle, they saw three things in it that would have suggested to them that Jesus was the long-expected Messiah.

To begin with, it took place in *the setting of a marriage*. The relationship between God and Israel had been frequently described as a marriage. True, the marriage had run into difficulties and their stormy relationship often led to a temporary parting of the ways. The prophet Hosea, among others, had captured something of the turbulent emotions involved. Yet the prophets looked forward to a time when the relationship would be repaired and set on the course of permanent renewal. Isaiah 54:5–7, for example, speaks in these terms:

Your Maker is your husband—the Lord Almighty is his name—the Holy One of Israel is your Redeemer; he is called the God of all the earth. The Lord will call you back as if you were a wife deserted and distressed in spirit—a wife who married young, only to be rejected… For a brief moment I abandoned you, but with deep compassion I will bring you back.

Isaiah 62:4–5 is another example where God speaks of rejoicing over his people 'as a bridegroom rejoices over his bride'. The setting was significant.

Then, there was *the abundant nature of the provision*. Far more water was turned into wine than was necessary to save the young couple's blushes. Why so much? Why so over the top? Because people expected that when the Messiah came, they would enter an age of abundance. Whenever God was truly at work, there was ample provision made. He never intended his creatures to eke out a meagre existence in his world. He richly resourced it. Abundance was a sign of his presence and a symbol of his blessing. As the prophets looked forward to the coming of the Messiah, they expected the trees to blossom, the corn to flourish and 'the bounty of the Lord' to be apparent (Hosea 14:7; Jeremiah 31:12). Amos, indeed, not only looked forward to that day as one when 'the reaper will be overtaken by the one who ploughs' because the harvest would take so long to gather in, but also, significantly, as a day when 'new wine will drip from the mountains and flow from all the hills' (Amos 9:13). With mounting excitement, the disciples began to believe that the day had arrived and the Messiah was present among them.

Finally, there was *the significance of the jars* used in the miracle. John tells us that these jars were 'the kind used by the Jews for ceremonial washing' (v. 6). Since strict Jews had to wash their hands at a meal between every course, they would have needed this number of massive jars to meet the guests' needs throughout the week. But when Jesus turned water into wine, the jars were no longer available to be used for ritual washing. His action signalled that the old ritual regulations were about to be replaced by the new kingdom of grace. It symbolized the end of the old way of maintaining God's favour by obedience to ritual law, and the provision of a new way of enjoying God through his mercy and grace being freely bestowed on our sinful and undeserving lives. It was a sign that the new age of the Messiah had come.

The disciples saw his glory in the miracle of transformation because they saw in it his claim to be the Messiah, his ushering in of the new age and his provision of grace. Here, indeed, is glory: glory to transform failure, to fill emptiness, to restore brokenness, to enrich barrenness, to release grace and to provide in abundance. But it is a glory that comes at a price—the price of the cross, as implied by Jesus' reference to 'my time' in his reply to his mother.

Questions

1. What does this event do to your image of God? Do you view him as a puritanical miser, watching all too cautiously over scarce resources, or as a bountiful and generous provider?

2. How would you answer Strauss's comment that this miracle seems to provide one couple with unnecessary luxury while ignoring the pitiful needs of much of the world? What do you make of a situation where God seems to pamper a few at the expense of the many?

4

The glory of the temple cleaner

JOHN 2:13–22

It was not generally considered as one of the most glorious moments of the British General Election in 2001 when the Deputy Prime Minister threw a punch at an angry bystander who jostled him in the crowd. Press and public alike thought his ill-tempered reaction to be shameful. So how can John possibly think that Jesus' violent cleansing of the temple was a revelation of his glory?

Before we go further, we must rid ourselves of the idea, which many of us picked up in Sunday school, that Jesus was an insipid, emotionless character whose reactions were always meek and mild. Philip Yancey put his finger on the problem when he wrote that he grew up believing that Jesus' personality matched that of the Vulcan Mr Spock in *Star Trek*: 'He remained calm, cool and collected as he strode like a robot among the excitable human beings on spaceship earth.' But, Yancey continues, 'that is not what I found in the gospels… Other people affected Jesus deeply: obstinacy frustrated him, self-righteousness infuriated him, simple faith thrilled him. Indeed, he seemed more emotional and spontaneous than the average person, not less. More passionate, not less.'[8]

Jesus was never more passionate than on the day he cleansed the temple. How did this display his glory? His actions revealed it in four ways.

What he abolished (vv. 12–16)

The business of the temple was to offer sacrifices so that people could be cleansed from their sin. At the special festivals, a mountain of sacrifices would be offered. Now sacrifices require animals, and animals require markets in which they can be purchased, and markets require money changers so that the purchases can be made—at least, they do when you have to buy them with special temple currency. A convenient mark-up of ten or twelve per cent was involved in changing the money, costing the average worshipper a couple of day's wages. But if the money changers profited from all this, they only did so, they would have said, because they were providing people with a helpful service.

That is why Jesus accuses them of turning the temple into a cave of bandits, alluding to Jeremiah 7:11: 'Has this house, which bears my Name, become a den of robbers to you? But I have been watching! declares the Lord.'

In casting out the market traders and money changers, the representatives of the sacrificial system, Jesus was cleansing the old order and abolishing the need for the endless, repetitive killing of animals, and all the exploitation that went with it, as a way of relating to God. He is saying that a new day, a day of grace, has dawned.

What he accomplished (v. 16)

Where did the traders carry out this commercial activity? They set up their booths and their pens in the temple precincts, in what was meant to be the Court of the Gentiles. The one place, then, where Gentiles could come to pray had to be turned into a market. The nearest place the Gentiles could get to the living presence of God had been filled with sheep and money exchangers. There was no room left for the Gentiles. Sorry, but the Gentiles were no longer welcome.

The Jewish religion of the day had become so twisted by a desire to offer pure worship that it excluded the Gentiles and kept them out. Jesus said, 'Enough! The day has come. It is time for the Father's house to be released so that it can be a house where all nations are welcome to pray.'

That was exactly what Isaiah had envisaged would happen when the Messiah came, as the other Gospels remind us. He foresaw a day when no foreigner who wanted to serve the Lord would be excluded from the temple, and when racial and ethnic distinctions would no longer matter. Rather, on that day God promised to bring 'foreigners who bind themselves to the Lord to serve him, to love the name of the Lord, and to worship him… to my holy mountain and give them joy in my house of prayer… for my house will be called a house of prayer for all nations' (Isaiah 56:6–7). So while, in C.H. Dodd's words, it was popularly expected that the Messiah '"would cleanse Jerusalem from the Gentiles", Jesus wanted it cleansed *for* the Gentiles'.[9]

Being a Gentile was not the only thing that made people unclean in Jewish eyes, so it was not the only thing to exclude people from temple worship. Those who were ritually impure were not welcome; nor were those who suffered some physical disability. But Jesus opened up access to God for them as well as the Gentiles. Matthew 21:14 suggests as much when, in its account of the cleansing of the temple, it adds the telling comment that 'the blind and the lame came to him *at the temple*, and he healed them'. Such a thing was unheard of. Such a thing would have aroused indignation in the hearts of the temple officials. Such a thing would have provoked hostility to Jesus and begun already to seal his fate.

What Jesus accomplished by this deed was to open up access to God for all by abolishing a religious system that cried out to many, 'Keep out!'

What he relinquished (v. 17)

As the disciples reflected on this incident, verse 17 tells us that another Old Testament scripture came into their minds. Psalm 69:9 includes the statement, 'Zeal for your house consumes me.' The psalm is the prayer of someone who is so dedicated to the Lord and to the honour of the temple that he finds himself rejected by his family and scorned by his friends. As they see the zeal that Jesus has for his Father's house, the disciples know that he will attract the same opprobrium and pay the same cost. This action, like so many of his others, paved the way to the cross. This heroic act did not require Jesus to have a modicum of courage; it required him to be prepared to relinquish his life.

The different strands of the story are closely woven together. One strand shows him abolishing the sacrificial system; this strand shows us why he could do so. He could abolish the old sacrificial system because he himself was to become the ultimate sacrifice. He could welcome the Gentiles and the unclean into the temple because he was going to pay for their entry with his own blood (Ephesians 2:13).

What he established (vv. 18–22)

The Jews naturally ask Jesus what authority he has for taking such action. 'What right have you? Prove yourself!' they demand. He gives them an answer, but it's an answer that leaves them more puzzled than they were before. He tells them that their temple would not only be cleansed and reformed but also totally destroyed... and then rebuilt in three days. 'What nonsense,' they thought. The Jews had started to build the temple in the year 19BC, and 46 years later it was still not complete. Its massive foundation stones, which were 30 feet long, and its 37-foot-high pillars had taken years to put in place. How, if it were destroyed, could it possibly be rebuilt in a couple of days?

Jesus' reply was a riddle. It contained not one but two messages about the future. It warned them that the day would come when God's judgment would finally descend upon them, and the temple, along with everything they stood for, would come crashing down around them. This part of the message came true when the Romans sacked Jerusalem, destroyed the temple and effectively brought the nation to an end in AD70. Jesus was admonishing them to prepare for the coming judgment.

But he was also alluding to his own future. From another angle, the temple of which he was speaking, John realized, was not the temple of stone and sacrificial altars, in which they were standing, but the temple of his own body. That temple, too, would be destroyed on a cross and three days later be rebuilt in the resurrection. Jesus was claiming that the existing physical temple, which had been at the heart of the Jewish nation's worship, was going to be abolished and replaced by a new centre of worship, namely himself.

Only at a superficial level is the cleansing of the temple about the danger of the commercialization of religion. More significantly, here we see the glory of the priest who truly cleansed, the Messiah who opened the way to God for all, the Son who suffered as the ultimate sacrifice and the prophet who predicted judgment and salvation to come. Before the voice of prophecy fell silent for 400 years, Malachi had forecast that 'suddenly the Lord you are seeking will come to his temple; the messenger of the covenant, whom you desire, will come' (3:1). As Jesus cleansed the temple, the disciples detected that Malachi's prophecy was being fulfilled before their eyes. The Lord had come.

Questions

1. Whom does the Church exclude from worship today, considering them to be the 'unclean'?

2. What does this incident do to the image of 'gentle Jesus meek and mild'? How far do you believe in a strong Jesus?

5

The glory of the wise teacher

JOHN 3:1–21

Early in life, Noel Smith was diagnosed with a serious heart condition. As a result, he led a severely restricted life and survived on a disability allowance. Then, when he was 59, he was told it had all been a mistake. The newspapers reported that he was bitter, and quoted him as saying, 'I have been told now that I can start to learn to live, but how do you do that after so many years?'[10] It was a fair question. It was also the question that Nicodemus, one of Israel's teachers, asked Jesus, 'the teacher who had come from God', late one night, after dark. Jesus' masterly reply demonstrates his glory by casting him in the role of a wise teacher.

The teacher's lesson (vv. 1–3)

The miraculous signs that Jesus performed had aroused Nicodemus' curiosity. He longed to know more about what made Jesus tick. At this time, Nicodemus was not yet a believer, even a secret believer, but a sympathetic Jewish seeker, in reality still living in darkness, as John symbolizes by his coming to Jesus at night. He approaches Jesus respectfully, but before Nicodemus can get beyond his initial greeting and pose a question, Jesus, brusquely upfront, sets before him the crucial lesson he wants to teach. 'I tell you the truth, no one can see the kingdom of God without being born again.' It's impossible, in other words, to be a true subject of God, living under his liberating rule, without starting a radically different life, starting all over again.

This was a shock to Nicodemus who, until that point, had believed otherwise. Nicodemus was from the top drawer of Jewish society and a member of the religious élite. He was one of the 6000 Pharisees and a member of the ruling council of Israel. This council was traditionally made up of 71 leading men, dominated by the high priest. Under the ultimate authority of Rome, it exercised spiritual and judicial authority in Judea. Nicodemus was a thoughtful and intelligent man who respected religion and observed the traditions of Israel. As a Pharisee, he would also have been scrupulous in keeping the law. Besides working hard not to break the law themselves, the Pharisees had a genuine desire to break it down into manageable, bite-sized pieces so that ordinary people could understand it and be encouraged to keep it. Surely he was more acceptable than most in God's kingdom? But Jesus says that privilege is not enough, religion is not enough, and morality is not enough to enable anyone to enter God's kingdom. From what Jesus goes on to say, he teaches Nicodemus that self-improvement and mere reformation are not enough. Only one thing will do it: rebirth.

The teacher's explanation (vv. 4–9)

A wise teacher captures his pupil's imagination right at the start of a lesson, and Jesus has certainly succeeded in doing that. A wise teacher will also go on patiently to explain what may initially be unclear to his class. Jesus does just that to the puzzled class of one that he has before him. Nicodemus asks, 'How can someone who is already old be born again?'

Jesus explains that there are two types of birth: the physical birth of a human baby, regularly associated with water, and the spiritual birth of someone as a child of God (already mentioned in John 1:12–13), associated with the work of the God's Spirit. The first birth is the work of human parents; the second is the initiative of the Spirit of God. Jesus' point is becoming plain. Just as a lamb doesn't give birth to a horse, so the physical does not give birth to the spiritual. Each operates within its own sphere. So Nicodemus needs to be twice-born. He has experienced the first birth but he has yet to experience the second. If he does not do so, then he will remain lifeless in relation to God and outside his kingdom.

Archbishop William Temple once explained it like this:

It is no good giving me a play like Hamlet *or* King Lear, *and telling me to write a play like that. Shakespeare could do it; I can't. And it is no good showing me a life like the life of Jesus and telling me to live a life like that. Jesus could do it; I can't. But if the genius of Shakespeare could come and live in me, then I could write plays like that. And if the Spirit of Jesus could come and live in me, then, I could live a life like that.*[11]

Just so, we can only live the twice-born life as members of the kingdom of God if the Spirit of God comes to live in us.

Jesus frankly admits that there is a mystery in this. Using a brilliant double entendre, he speaks of not knowing where the wind comes from or where it's going, but nonetheless being fully aware of its effect. He is using word play, because the word for 'wind' in Greek (and in Hebrew) can also mean 'breath' or 'spirit'. In Genesis 2:7, God's spirit breathes the 'breath of life' into Adam. So God now mysteriously, sovereignly, breathes life again into those who believe in his Son.

It is all deeply disturbing for Nicodemus. As Tom Wright comments, 'Opening the window and letting the breeze in can be very inconvenient, especially for the Nicodemuses of this world who suppose they have got things tidied up, labelled and sorted.'[12]

The teacher's authority (vv. 10–15)

What develops next is a discussion on Jesus' authority—that is, both the authority that qualifies him to teach and the authority he exercises as a teacher.

When someone sets themselves up as a teacher, you want to know what qualifications they have for doing so. How can you trust that they know what they are talking about? How confident can you be that they truly have a good grasp of the subject? Nicodemus, after all, was meant to be a teacher in Israel and he was stumped by the teaching of Jesus. So, what is Jesus' authority?

It is a question that will occupy much attention in John's Gospel. Briefly introduced at this point, we learn that Jesus has the authority of experience. He speaks of things that he knows because he has seen them. And he has seen them because of where he comes from—that is, from the other world, from heaven, the dwelling place of God himself.

Who he is and where he comes from give him authority in the second sense, namely authority to exercise power over those whom he teaches. It is an authority that he longs to use for good. Reminding Nicodemus of the incident in the wilderness when the Israelites were punished by God for their grumbling and then healed only if they looked to a snake that Moses had erected on a pole (the story is mentioned in Numbers 21), Jesus says that his role is like that of the snake. He has the authority to bring new life to all who look to him. But, like the snake, he can only do so if he is 'lifted up'—not on a pole but on a cross. His, then, is a costly authority to exercise, an authority that brings life to others at the expense of his own life.

The teacher's impact (vv. 16–21)

Teachers often have a lasting impact, for good or ill, on those they teach. Through them, students are either well prepared or ill prepared for life. They have a hand in shaping the destiny of those they have taught. Yet no teacher has ever had a fraction of the impact of the wise teacher from Nazareth. He has shaped the destiny of countless millions—all, in fact, who have ever lived.

The conversation between Jesus and Nicodemus gives way to

John's own reflections, probably around verse 16. From then on, John sets out a series of contrasts that show the impact this teacher can have on those who believe in him. We either have eternal life or we perish. We either experience salvation or we are subject to condemnation. We either embrace the light or we continue to live in darkness. We either live by the truth or we stumble around, basing our lives on lies.

The wise teacher from Nazareth does more than just getting a few ideas into people's heads, and more than opening up a world that uninstructed eyes have not yet seen. He makes it possible, in his own person, for people to start life all over again. He makes it possible for people to leave behind the past, to break free from the hurts that have shaped them or the powers that have oppressed them or the failures of which they are ashamed, and to shake off the shallow existence of life without God. This teacher gives his students the gifts not of education, but of life, salvation, light and truth: 'For God so loved the world that he gave his one and only Son, that whoever believes in him shall not perish but have eternal life.' What a glorious teacher!

Questions

1. The phrase 'born again' tends to have negative overtones for many today, influenced by media stereotypes. How can we reclaim the phrase and restore some of Jesus' original meaning to it?

2. Look back at this extraordinarily rich passage. What struck you about it that the notes above didn't comment on? What would you have highlighted from the teaching of Jesus?

6

The glory of the expected bridegroom

JOHN 3:22–36

Some best men fail in their duties. When James Cripps, a Bristol University student, was on holiday abroad with his best man a few years ago, he got drunk and, in an inebriated state, married a total stranger. His best man failed to stop him. Returning home, he confessed his error to his fiancée, who failed to see the funny side of the story and promptly ditched him.[13] It is the task of the best man to protect the bridegroom and to do so without attracting attention to himself.

Building on the familiar Old Testament picture of God as the bridegroom and Israel as the bride, John the Baptist resorts to the image of the 'friend who attends the bridegroom' to describe his own role in relation to 'the Christ'. Three important issues arise from what he says.

The centrality of the bridegroom (vv. 22–30)

John the Baptist's disciples were getting worried. Faced with the rising popularity of Jesus, they feared that the crowds were deserting John and going after Jesus instead. Surely John would have been jealous of Jesus' success and envious of his competition. Could he not take some action to ensure that he remained high in the popularity stakes? John's reply is deeply revealing about the nature of Christian service and full of wisdom.

It speaks to us, first of all, about *the prerequisite of ministry*. 'A person can receive only what is given from heaven' (v. 27). Those who want to serve God must accept the role that God gives them to play. It is impossible to force God's hand to be given a greater role than the one that he, in his sovereignty, has assigned. We cannot exercise any successful ministry beyond the sphere of influence or the allotted time that God has determined, however hard we try.

It speaks to us, secondly, about *the function of ministry*. 'The bride belongs to the bridegroom' (v. 29). The role of the best man is not to be a hindrance to their relationship but to lead the bride and groom together. His remit is to protect the interests of the groom. To put himself between them, to flirt with the bride and, however subtly, to woo her away from her intended husband is shameful. Some ancient laws treated it as a heinous crime. In former days, the British would describe a person who did this as a cad.

Paul makes use of a variation on this theme in 2 Corinthians 11:2, when he mercilessly exposes the dangerous seduction of false apostles: 'I am jealous for you with a godly jealousy. I promised you to one husband, to Christ, so that I might present you as a pure virgin to him.' Woe betide any who get in the way and distract attention from the bridegroom, whether by false teaching or well-meaning but self-glorifying strategies of mission, or by empire building rather than by truly building Christ's Church.

It speaks to us, thirdly, about *the implications of ministry*. 'He must become greater; I must become less' (v. 30). If the centre stage is to be occupied by the bridegroom, it means that the best man has to move to one side. In John's case, he knows that great humility is called for so that the spotlight can move away from him and increasingly shine on Jesus. Before long, he will move off the stage altogether; his role will be over and his job of introducing Jesus done. Few of us find this as easy as it seems. We so easily fall prey to the ravenous temptations of pride, envy and jealousy. We want to keep people's attention focused on us rather than on Christ. C.S.

Lewis was right when he wrote, 'There is one vice of which no man in the world is free... The vice I am talking about is pride... Pride leads to every other vice: it is the complete anti-God state of mind... Pride is a spiritual cancer.'[14] John Stott was equally right to say, 'Nothing is more hostile to spiritual growth than arrogance, and nothing more conducive to spiritual growth than humility.'[15]

The origin of the bridegroom (vv. 31–32)

The gossip that goes on at weddings is amazing! I know—I've heard a great deal of it in the weddings I have conducted over the years. The assorted distant relatives and friends who gather love to chat about the happy couple. 'Did you know...?' 'She earns more than he does, you know...' 'He's been married before, you know...' Here John tells us two things about the origin of the bridegroom he serves.

First, John points to *the superiority of his origin*. Where did Jesus come from? Where did he really originate? What was his background? Unlike any other human being, John asserts, he is 'the one who comes from above' and consequently 'is above all'. The rest of us ordinary mortals are 'from the earth'. We come from the dust of the ground and inherit our genes from our parents. Our knowledge and understanding of God and his world, therefore, are necessarily limited and distorted—but Jesus Christ comes from outside and does not suffer from such limitations. He is omniscient and intimate with God because he comes from above. When he speaks of God, then, he speaks of what he knows and says what comes naturally to him. All this testifies to his supremacy. No human being surpasses him, nor could any ever do so.

Second, John points to *the superiority of his testimony*. If he is 'from above', he is speaking about things 'he has seen and heard'. He is engaged not in speculation but in revelation. He deals not in conjecture but in certainty. He does not try to put the confusing pieces of life's experience together to make sense of them, as if completing a jigsaw. He designed the jigsaw. He is not seeking to unravel a mystery. He is the mystery who makes himself known. He does not blindly grope his way towards God, since he has come from God. Jesus speaks with the authority of one from above. How odd, then, as John remarks, that 'no one accepts his testimony'.

The mission of the bridegroom (vv. 34–36)

Having explained why we should pay attention to Jesus, John goes on to enumerate the gifts that this bridegroom brings. He speaks *the truth of God*. Certainly, his words sound strange, odd, even hard. He speaks upside-down words about loving enemies, the first being last, losing one's life to find it, the unclean really being acceptable, insiders being the true outsiders, and about the error of parading one's piety before others. They are words from another world about another kingdom, about another, eternal way of life, yet his words exercise a magnetic power over people. Weird though they may be to a common way of thinking, people realize that they make sense about the way we should be living. In turning the world upside down, they actually turn the world the right way up. They are words, as John Bunyan said, that are 'short, precise, terrible *and* full of refreshment'. That's because they are true—as they must be, since they have their origin in the God who cannot lie.

Jesus embodies *the Spirit of God*, because in him 'God gives the Spirit without limit'. In Jesus, we not only hear the words of God but also see what a human life would look like when full of the Holy Spirit. No other human being has ever possessed the Spirit in such complete measure. Being full of the Spirit empowered Jesus for mission, sanctified him for living, energized him for self-giving and safeguarded him so that the intimate relationship of the Trinity was not fractured.

The life that Jesus enjoys with God is not one that he keeps to himself, however, for he transmits *the life of God* to others who put their trust in him. He is the channel through whom a new quality of existence flows, a new meaning and a new centre of life are discovered, as we are restored in our relationship with God. It is described as 'eternal life', which serves as an appropriate description in itself and a fitting way of distinguishing it from ordinary living, in which people have never experienced reconciliation with God.

The benefits of Christ are negative as well as positive, for he averts *the wrath of God*. John's way of speaking is stark, constantly employing sharp contrasts. Elsewhere he speaks of living in the light or in darkness. Here, he says that we either have eternal life or we don't. And if we haven't got it, then we are living under the continuing wrath of God—a wrath that is the inevitable result of living in sin. But the Son who comes to bring life averts God's wrath by bearing our sin and its consequences in his own person and settling our accounts on his cross. That's why people need to be introduced to the bridegroom—so that they can enjoy eternal life now, experiencing the Spirit for themselves, walking in truth every day and being sure of enjoying God's acceptance at the end.

Here we see the glory of the bridegroom who came to capture his bride and bestow on her a multitude of undeserved and life-giving gifts. Those who are his 'friends' must assist in the process, but dare not get in the way. As John said, so they must say, 'He must become greater; I must become less.' The glory is all his.

Questions

1. Is there a danger that the contemporary Church abuses its position and attracts attention to itself as the best man, rather than attracting attention to Jesus?

2. John uses wedding imagery again in Revelation 19:6–8. How do those verses develop the teaching of John 3?

7

The glory of the thirst quencher

JOHN 4:1–42

The social commentator Robert Putnam has summed up the character of contemporary American society in the epithet 'bowling alone'. A nation that was once held together by strong extended families and a network of voluntary associations, where people were rooted in healthy communities, has disintegrated into a society of isolated, lonely individuals where people go 'bowling alone'.[16] The epithet has caught on because so many can see how true to life it is.

The woman Jesus met in Sychar was not so much bowling alone as drawing water alone. Since the society in which Jesus lived was not one where people would have usually done anything on their own, let alone go to fetch water in the middle of the day (usually a communal activity undertaken at a cooler hour), we are immediately alerted to something unusual going on. The long conversation that follows reveals a great deal about this unnamed woman and her circumstances but, even more, it reveals, yet again, the glory of Jesus.

He is the supplier of living water (vv. 4–18)

The fact that the conversation ever took place at all is amazing. No wonder she was surprised when Jesus spoke to her! They were divided by gender, race, theology and history. He was a man, she a woman. He was a Jew, she a Samaritan. He subscribed to the whole

Old Testament, she only to the Pentateuch, the first five books of the Bible. For 400 years there had been tension between their nations. For a Jewish male to speak like this to a Samaritan women was highly irregular, indeed highly suspect. Since women were considered a source of great temptation, some serious Pharisees would not even acknowledge their wives in the street, let alone speak to any other female. Perhaps this is why John says, somewhat curiously, that Jesus 'had to go through Samaria'. There was no 'had to' about it, since good Jews would have just walked the long way round from Jerusalem to Galilee and avoided Samaria, unless it was the 'had to' of divine compulsion.

As if talking with her isn't enough to induce a heart attack, it's not long before Jesus throws her further off balance by offering her 'living water'. No wonder she was confused, as she was the one who had the bucket! But, of course, he doesn't mean ordinary water that quenches physical thirst. That water only ever satisfies for a time, and then a further drink is needed. He means the water that is a gift of God, which has the power to quench the deepest thirsts of the soul, eternally. And when it came to that kind of thirst, this woman was thirsty indeed.

Here was a woman who was longing to be loved. She had been, it emerged, married to five different husbands and was currently on her own. Even the liberal Jewish rabbis didn't approve of a woman having more than three husbands. So she was probably a stigmatized woman in her village (that probably explains why she was drawing water on her own at the height of the day)—but we shouldn't assume it was her fault. Who knows how those men treated her and whether their neglect or abuse was not the cause of her problems? Whatever the reason, it had left her with an aching void. She was running on empty. Her frequent marriages were, more than likely, an attempt to fill the emptiness, but her situation brought Jeremiah's words to mind: 'My people have committed two sins: they have forsaken me, the spring of living water, and have dug their own cisterns, broken cisterns that cannot hold water' (Jeremiah 2:13).

Perhaps she kept the ache to herself, as many people do, afraid that there is no answer. In Ann Graham Lotz's poetic words, however, Jesus knows 'the small secrets of your heart, the unspoken dreams of your imagination, the unrevealed thoughts of your mind, the emotional shards of your feelings, the paralysing fears for your future, the bitter resentments of your past'.[17] And he can quench the thirst of them all. As he quite legitimately promised, 'those who drink the water I give them will never thirst. Indeed, the water I give them will become in them a spring of water welling up to eternal life' (v. 14).

Jesus' solution, unlike many of the other 'sticking plaster' solutions that are on offer, goes deep. Before she can drink of this living water, the woman has to face up to the truth about herself and her situation. That's why Jesus tells her to go and call her husband. Her past needs dealing with, not burying. She needs to confess the mistakes and so receive the forgiveness that God bestows. There is no cure without undergoing the operation.

The glory of Jesus is seen as he quenches the yearning of this woman's soul.

He is the centre of true worship (vv. 19–26)

We must not move to the conclusion too fast! Having been confronted with personal issues about her past, she tries a well-known diversionary tactic to lessen the embarrassment. She flatters him ('Sir, I can see you are a prophet'), and then seeks to engage him in an academic theological argument. That should be safe enough territory. She raises the issue that had caused the dispute between their nations 400 years before. Based on questionable interpretations of the books of Moses, the Samaritans refused to worship at the temple on Mount Zion and built their own shrine on Mount Gerizim. Which mountain, she wonders, is the right one?

Jesus doesn't answer the question directly. Instead, he shifts the ground completely. He reveals that, from now on, people will worship 'neither on this mountain nor in Jerusalem'. God will not be found in the shrines that had been built there but will be found, instead, in Jesus himself. It is a person, not a place, that is important. He will be the new centre of worship.

In expanding on his answer a little, Jesus teaches some other things about worship that are vital if we want to be 'the kind of worshippers the Father seeks'. Not all worship is acceptable to God. Jesus' verdict on Samaritan worship was that it was misguided and ignorant, and the same could be said of much that passes for worship today. His point is that acceptable worship is well based on the truth that God has made known in the whole sweep of scripture, not on selective and distorted bits, still less on our own ideas and vain imaginings. It is also worship in which heart and mind, spirit and truth, the inward attitude as well as the outward actions, are consistently in harmony with one another.

But then Jesus says the most amazing thing of all, as she tries to continue to spar with him in theological discussion. As a Samaritan, and hence one who would have known the Pentateuch, she knows on the basis of Deuteronomy 18:15 that a prophet like Moses, only greater, will come one day. So she concedes that all the questions about worship will be sorted out when the Messiah comes. Jesus' reply to her is stunning: 'I who speak to you am he.' Here is the most explicit claim made by Jesus in the Gospels about his true identity, and he ventures it to this disreputable woman who is a member of a tainted nation. John does not immediately record her reaction.

He is the Saviour of the world (vv. 25–26, 39–42)

The best punchlines come at the very end. When a comedian lets the punchline slip halfway through a joke, he or she risks ridicule by the audience. John's account of Jesus' visit to Sychar is certainly no joke, but the punch line does come right at the end.

Whatever the woman's initial reaction to Jesus' claim to be the Messiah, the blinkers must soon have fallen off her eyes, for when she comes back into the story she is accompanied by the rest of her village, to whom she has been chatting. Somehow she has persuaded them that this Jesus is worth checking out and, when they do so, they come to believe in him as the Messiah for themselves. And here's the punchline: 'we know that this man really is the Saviour of the world'.

The glory of Jesus lies not only in his unique ability to quench the deepest thirsts of our lives, justifiably making him the focus of our adoration and object of our worship, but in his ability to be a universal Saviour. He quenches the thirst not just of Jews, but of Samaritans too; not just of men, but of women too; not just of the deserving, but of the undeserving; not just of the reasonably moral, but of the disreputable. There is no one who lies outside the Saviour's embrace and no one whose thirst he cannot quench.

Questions

1. What are the deep, even hidden, thirsts in your life? Have you admitted them to Jesus and allowed him to deal with them? Remember, his treatment of them will be profound, not a quick-fix therapy.

2. Reflect on what is at the centre of your worship. Does it revolve around Jesus, or around a building, a piece of symbolism, a style of music or a tradition?

8

The glory of the distant healer

JOHN 4:43–54

When you live in London (I speak from personal experience), you are apt to think that all the action takes place there. Nothing significant happens elsewhere, especially in some small village remote from the centre of power. They felt a bit like that in Jerusalem during the time Jesus was alive, yet it was in the remote backwater of Cana that Jesus revealed his glory not once, but twice. The best that could be said of Cana was that it produced good spring water but, situated five miles from Nazareth on the road from Tiberias, there was little else there. It was a convenient stopping-off place on the road home from Jerusalem, where Jesus had just been. Perhaps he had family there—hence the wedding— and called to see them. Whatever the reason, this insignificant place was to be the setting where he performed his second faith-inducing sign. It didn't actually take place there, but… well, that's part of the point.

The glory of his compassion

Whenever Jesus encountered people who were carrying the grave hurts of life, compassion flowed out of him. His second miraculous sign demonstrates the point in a surprising way.

Here is compassion for *a man who was different*. The story concerns a 'royal official' who was based in Capernaum, some 20 miles away. He was probably in Cana on business. The description means that he was a senior civil servant, almost certainly a high-ranking military officer. Little else is known of him, although it is often suggested that the way he is introduced means that he was probably a member of Herod the tetrarch's inner circle. (Herod the tetrarch was Herod the Great's youngest son, who governed Galilee for Rome: see Luke 3:1.) The official may well have been a Gentile. Some even speculate that he may have been Chuza, the husband of Joanna, who is mentioned in Luke 8:3, but we cannot be sure. Given his position, he was unlikely to have been a practising Jew or even a very religious man at all. He didn't come from the ranks of the marginalized, among whom Jesus usually worked.

Here is compassion for *a man who was desperate*. Whatever the precise details of his public status, the official was first and foremost a father, and his son was not only ill but 'close to death'. Suffering is no respecter of persons. Pain touches all sorts of people. The anguish of human heartache exempts no class of family from its embrace. Wealth and status may occasionally make pain easier to bear, but they can alleviate it only in the most superficial of ways. Here was a father who was desperate to see his son's life saved and health restored.

Here is compassion for *a man who was determined*. Jesus' arrival caused a public commotion in Galilee, and it wasn't long before this royal official seized the opportunity to get Jesus on his case. Jesus' initial response is not encouraging. He seems wearied by the incessant quest for another miracle, another sensation that will entertain and titillate but not lead to real faith. So, to begin with, the official is rebuffed with a dismissive comment about sensation seekers, but he is not to be put off so easily. Like the Greek woman whom Jesus met while visiting Tyre (Mark 7:24–30), he is not dissuaded by Jesus' rebuff. Rather, it spurs him on and, refusing to stand on his dignity, he pleads again for his son's life with urgency and determination. Seeing that, Jesus immediately responds, speaks a word and, from a distance, issues the command for the boy to be healed.

Ben Witherington III has commented that 'we are meant to see the progress of a soul in this story, for while the official comes on the basis of Jesus' reputation as a miracle worker he leaves on the basis of a trust in Jesus' word *without* seeing a miracle or validating sign that his son would be all right'.[18] Here is true faith. It is a marvellous illustration of the way John White once defined faith when he wrote, 'Faith is the means by which Christians do business beyond time and space and bring to pass otherwise unrealizable hopes.'[19]

The glory of his power

Before we dwell too much on the response of the happy family, let's not lose sight of the power of the Lord. He only spoke a sentence and a miracle took place, 20 miles away and 700 feet below the level where Jesus was standing.

It was only a few words—'Your son will live'—but they were *effective words*. The son immediately got well. Here is a convincing demonstration that the claim made in the Prologue to the Gospel, that Jesus was the creating, life-giving Word, was neither an empty one nor merely a theoretical one. Here is John 1:1 being put into effect in a real-life (or rather life-and-death) situation.

His words were *life-restoring words*. Three times, in verses 50, 51 and 53, the accent falls on life. This too reflects John 1 and the claim made there that 'in him was life, and that life was the light of all people'. A faith healer on BBC News recently said, 'People can be complete atheists, they can believe in toffee apples, it wouldn't make any difference at all. Spiritual healing is like switching on an electric light. The power is there; it happens whether you have faith or not.' John would beg to differ. The healing does not flow from some impersonal force but from a person, the one who is our Creator and the source of all life. It was when he spoke that things changed, broken lives were healed and captive sinners were set free. It is worth noticing that the words Jesus spoke were not only effective but *precise words*. When the official asked his servants when his son had got better, he discovered that it was at the exact time when Jesus was pronouncing his words of restoration. Given such precision, it would be difficult to dismiss this miracle as a coincidence. There could be no shadow of doubt that Jesus was responsible for what happened, even though he was nowhere near the sickly lad when the healing took place. When Jesus healed, he never improved people's condition just a little bit. His words did exactly what he wanted them to, when he wanted them to, and the effects were clearly demonstrable and open to be examined by others.

His words were also *faith-building words*. The effect of this miracle, like the effect of the first miracle to be performed in Cana, was that people came to recognize who he was and to trust in him. The new believers were not found this time among the inner circle of Jesus' friendship group but in the outer circle of an official's household, who lived some distance away. John speaks of their faith in a characteristically absolute way. He says, in a simple, unqualified way, 'they believed'. In this straightforward manner, they trusted in Jesus without 'ifs' and 'buts'. From this time on, they had an irrevocable commitment to him, to follow in his ways. Like John and the other disciples, they too had seen his glory, and the only way to respond appropriately was to put faith in him.

The two miraculous signs that John has reported up until this point in his Gospel have a number of things in common, but equally exhibit a number of differences. One is a miracle performed on water, the other a miracle performed on a person. Jesus is Lord of nature and of people. One takes place right where they are standing, the other at a great distance. He is Lord both near and far. One takes place in person, the other by proxy. He is Lord of those who call on him and of those who don't.

Think, too, what they have in common. They both take place in Cana. They both respond to genuine need. They both involve a word of command by Jesus. They both result in people exercising faith in him. And they both reveal his glory—a glory of compassion and power combined in perfect harmony.

✛

Questions

1. Read Genesis 1 and Psalm 33:1–11. God speaks and life is created. Jesus spoke and life was granted. Is that why people began to see Jesus as God?

2. The glory of Jesus was revealed because one man had a bold and determined faith. Would we see more of the glory of Jesus if we had such faith? Pray about specific situations where you may be called upon to exercise real faith today.

The glory of the Sabbath breaker

JOHN 5:1–15

It was festival time when Jesus performed his third sign, and he was back in Jerusalem. Wandering the streets, as tourists and pilgrims do, Jesus and his disciples found themselves in the north-east corner of the city at the pool of Bethesda. The name means something like 'house of outpouring'. In fact, it was two pools and was surrounded by five colonnades that can still be seen today. The pools were fed from large reservoirs and underneath there were springs that occasionally erupted. The resulting disturbances gave rise to the idea that an angel was troubling the water and that, when he did so, the water temporarily had healing qualities. The first person into the water would benefit from its restorative powers.

Such was the setting for Jesus' third miracle, a miracle performed on one of the least attractive people in the Gospel. It is a story full of the perversity of human beings, but, in spite of it all, Jesus' glory shines.

Jesus takes the initiative (vv. 3–6)

Around the pool lay many disabled people waiting for the waters to be disturbed, in the hope of healing. But John is emphatic: 'One who was there…' Why did Jesus choose this one to heal and ignore the rest? The man had not asked to be cured and, judging by his response to Jesus, perhaps he didn't even want to be. We do not really know why Jesus took the initiative with this one man. Jesus, we read, 'learned that he had been in this condition for a long time'. Did someone tell Jesus? Was that how he found out? Probably not. The word 'learned' probably gives a more definite impression than the original suggests. It really means, 'when Jesus knew... discovered... became aware of'. It does not imply that the source of his knowledge was what other people told him. In fact, John might be suggesting that Jesus had a supernatural knowledge of the man's condition. He had certainly shown superhuman perception before (see 1:47–48; 4:17–18) and, as the Creator of human beings, knew what was in them (2:25).

Jesus asks a question (vv. 6–7)

His perception of the inner state of this man led Jesus to pose a deeply revealing question: 'Do you want to get well?' We might have thought the answer was obvious. What else was he doing there? Who wouldn't want to get well? But the way the man replies suggests that Jesus had touched a raw nerve. Don Carson says that his reply was 'the crotchety grumblings of an old and not very perceptive man who thinks he is answering a stupid question'.[20] He doesn't immediately say, 'Of course' or 'Yes, please'. He seems less than enthusiastic about the idea and full of self-pity. For him to be healed after 38 years of coping with his disability would take some adjustment. Pious Jews gave alms to people like him. Healing would involve an immediate loss of income. How would he cope? Some people (but certainly not all) who suffer a prolonged illness begin, over time, to find their identity through their illness. People notice and serve them because of their incapacity. It even gives them a certain status. To be made well might, after the initial period of rejoicing is past, involve a certain loss of attention, a reversion to ordinariness. The man's response here seems to suggest that he was emotionally as well as physically paralysed. Jesus' question, directed to his will, was exactly on target.

Jesus issues a command (vv. 8–9)

It is just as well that God does not always treat us as we deserve, or this man would probably never have been healed. Undeflected by the invalid's self-absorbed mumblings, Jesus commands him, 'Get up! Pick up your mat and walk.' Whether his action ca ɩe out of shock at the forcefulness of Jesus' words—it was unlikely to be out of faith—he did just that. Probably no one was more surprised than he was.

Archbishop William Temple said that the story is about the ability of Christ to restore lost powers in our lives. The man had lost the power to walk and hence to enjoy life.[21] In restoring the power to walk, Jesus also gave him the power to live again. Temple concluded, 'Our fellowship with Christ not only hallows and intensifies all the powers we have when we first meet with Him. It restores those which are atrophied by neglect or abuse. It is part of the deadly quality of sin that it hinders us from seeking a cure.'

The man may not have been genuinely seeking a cure but Jesus overcomes all the obstacles and, by his life-giving order, effects one. The fact that the man took up his mattress and walked was evidence of the order's genuineness.

Jesus breaks a law (vv. 9–12)

Just when you think the story is over, John says something that he clearly sees as very significant, which gives the story a new lease of life: 'The day on which this took place was a Sabbath.' What follows makes us think that this might be the real point of the third sign.

Keeping the Sabbath was crucial to all good Jews, along with circumcision and obedience to the food laws. It made them distinctive from others and preserved Judaism from compromise and erosion. Sabbath observance had become a priority because of passages like Jeremiah 17:19–27 and Nehemiah 13:15–19. Since these passages referred more to general principles than specific situations, Jewish teachers had subsequently tried to be helpful to ordinary folk by spelling out their meaning and application in more detail. So, by Jesus' day, people were required to keep 39 specific regulations if they were not to fall foul of the law. It was one of these regulations that the healed man broke when he carried his mat home from the pool of Bethesda. But it raises the question of whether he was really breaking the law of God or merely the traditions of human beings.

Initially (v. 10), the charge of Sabbath breaking is directed to the man who has been healed. He just passes the responsibility on to Jesus: 'The man who healed me made me do it. He's responsible.' This leads, in verse 18, to Jesus himself being accused of breaking the law, and quite a conversation follows, which we explore later.

Jesus would have been aware of the hostility that his action would provoke. So why did he do it on the Sabbath, apparently with calculated deliberation? After all, the man had been ill for 38 years. Surely one more day would not have mattered?

The other Gospels record Jesus regularly running into trouble on this issue and explain why he challenged this particular law so often, in a number of ways. On one occasion, Mark gives us two different but related explanations: Jesus said, 'The Sabbath was made for people, not people for the Sabbath. So the Son of Man is Lord even of the Sabbath' (Mark 2:27–28). How dare sincere but misguided teachers take a law that God had intended to be for the health and well-being of people and make it into an instrument of oppression! Jesus had come to release people from such petty legalism and, as the messianic Lord, he had the authority to do so. His action was signalling that the age of the Messiah had dawned, when people could enter permanently into a true rest, not just once a week into a temporary one. *He* is the Sabbath rest for which they longed.

In John, the point is somewhat different. Jesus, in verse 17, uses the incident to connect his work in giving life closely to the work of his Father as Creator of all. Putting himself on the same level with God leads to a new level of hostility between himself and the Jewish authorities. From now on, conflict, not curiosity, is going to dog his footsteps.

Jesus confronts the man (vv. 13–15)

We are getting ahead of ourselves. As soon as the man is healed, Jesus, as he often did, absents himself from the scene. He does so to save himself for another day. To have stayed around after such a miracle would have led either to being seized and instantly proclaimed Messiah or being seized by the authorities and locked up.

Although Jesus moves off quickly, it still seems utterly extraordinary that the man who has been healed makes no effort to enquire who has cured him. The man had no idea who Jesus was. There appears to be no shred of gratitude on his part, nor any hint of developing faith. He just took the gift of healing and ran.

When he and Jesus meet up again, Jesus takes the opportunity to warn him, 'Stop sinning.' Jesus makes clear elsewhere that there is not always a connection between sin and suffering (John 9:2–3), but sometimes they are closely tied. In view of Jesus' words here, this man's suffering does seem to have been caused originally by sin. Perhaps that was part of the divine knowledge that Jesus had of him at the beginning. So the command to stop sinning has a sense of urgency about it.

The story is uncomfortably realistic about human nature, but in it we see the glory of Jesus as he offers grace for the graceless, wholeness for the broken, freedom for the rule-bound, and rest for the weary.

Questions

1. Are there hurts in your life that you do not want Jesus to heal because you do not want to let go of them?

2. Look up Colossians 2:16–23 and Hebrews 4:1–11. What do they teach Christians about the Sabbath? How does such teaching add to the glory of Jesus?

10

The glory of the apprenticed son

JOHN 5:16–47

You'd think people would be delighted that a disabled man had been set on his feet again, but all that followed the healing of the man at the pool of Bethesda was an argument. What an anticlimax! What sparked the dispute was that Jesus had committed the heinous crime of healing on a Sabbath day. But although the quarrel may have been disappointing, it gave Jesus the opportunity to explain himself.

At first sight, the account Jesus gives about himself seems involved and complex. How are we to make sense of it? Tom Wright has given us a helpful clue. He uses the figure of the apprentice to help us understand what Jesus is saying.[22] My own father was an apprentice when he left school and worked for a period beside an experienced, qualified person who taught him a trade. It was a relationship between a master and a novice. Like all good metaphors and illustrations, the image shouldn't be pressed too far, as it does not always fit, but that's roughly how Jesus describes his work and relationship with his Father.

The apprentice's relationship (vv. 16–23)

Whether an apprenticeship is going to be a good one or not depends on the quality of relationship between the master and the student. If that dynamic is not right, the apprentice is likely to learn little. Where there is respect, harmony and trust, much will be learned. When Jesus comes to explain to the fault-finding Jews who he is, and therefore why he has the right to perform a miracle on the Sabbath, he starts by talking about his relationship with his Father.

First, it is *a relationship of equals* (vv. 16–18). The Jews readily acknowledged that God did not rest on the Sabbath in the sense of being inactive or taking a holiday. The very idea is absurd, for God must go on upholding and running his universe, even on the Sabbath, or else it will collapse in upon itself. If he were to withdraw his common grace towards creation, even for a day, it would cease to function. But he doesn't. The rabbis even said, 'May not a man walk through his house on the Sabbath? The heavens above and the earth below are God's house.' The Creator and life-giving God somehow had freedom from the Sabbath laws as Jewish tradition interpreted them. In the same way that God gives life and sustains his creation whether it is the Sabbath or not, Jesus (so he asserts) has the freedom to restore life to a broken man on the Sabbath.

Had they heard him correctly? Had Jesus just put himself on a level with the Lord God, King of the universe? The answer is an emphatic 'yes'. He was, they rightly discerned, claiming to be in a category all of his own in his relationship to the Father and was 'making himself equal with God' (v. 18). No wonder their hostility was to move up a gear! No one had ever claimed equality with God and got away with it.

Second, it is *a relationship of dependence* (v. 19). For all the Father and the Son have in common, the relationship is also marked by submission on the part of the Son. The Son exercises no independent authority in his own right. He is neither self-governing nor self-sufficient. All that he does, he does because he imitates his Father and acts in obedience to his Father's will. They act, as it were, in tandem with each other, one in heaven and the other on earth.

Third, it is *a relationship of love* (v. 20). Lest, in the light of the last comment, there should be any thought that the relationship that Jesus has with his Father is one of unhappy or enforced servility,

Jesus next explains that the relationship is one of love. Of the several Greek words that John could have chosen to express what Jesus said, the one he selects on this occasion is *philia*, the one that emphasizes love arising out of personal affection—and the love is mutual.

Fourth, it is *a relationship of trust* (vv. 21–22). If apprentices are to learn for themselves, there must come a point when they stop simply observing and start doing. The master must step back and entrust his pupils with the tools, the raw materials and the problems and let them find the answers for themselves. There can be no true learning without trust. God, we discover, has entrusted his Son with some awesome responsibilities, without abdicating his own sovereignty. He entrusts the Son, on the one hand, to provide life and, on the other hand, to pronounce judgment. Where the comparison with ordinary apprentices breaks down is that, to begin with, they risk making a mess of what is entrusted to them, whereas Jesus never learns by making mistakes. His gifts of salvation and his exercise of judgment are perfect from the start.

Fifth, it is *a relationship of honour* (v. 23). The honour and reputation of the master are always bound up with those of the student. If the apprentice acts shamefully, it reflects on the teacher. If one is honoured, so (indirectly, at least) is the other. The relationship between Father and Son is so close that to honour the one is to honour the other; to slight the one is to slight the other. It matters, therefore, how people respond to Jesus, for the way they respond to him is, in reality, the way they are responding to God himself.

The apprentice's responsibilities (vv. 24–47)

Without wishing to stretch the metaphor too far, we may ask what was the divine 'trade' that Jesus was entering. What were the responsibilities that his Father was passing on to him?

He was engaged in life-giving (vv. 24–26). John's Gospel has already taught us to think of Jesus as the life-giver. The opening chapter put it on the agenda. Then, in the early chapters, we read of him talking to a religious man about the need to start life again, through the mysterious operation of the Spirit. Next came a woman who had inwardly died but was brought to life again through the living water he offered her. Then we saw him working miracles that provided a dying boy and a disgruntled lame man with renewed physical life. On and on through the Gospel comes a parade of people to whom Jesus physically or spiritually, outwardly or inwardly, gives a new life—a new quality of life, eternal life, a foretaste of resurrection life. On it goes until the time comes for him to lay down his own life. Then the life-giver dies—until the third day, the day of indomitable resurrection life.

He was entrusted with judgment (vv. 27–30). Some people reject Jesus' life-restoring overtures and place themselves under the wrath of God. Instead of experiencing God's salvation, they experience his judgment. But this responsibility for judgment has also been entrusted to the Son. He is competent to judge 'because he is the Son of Man', meaning that he too has been a human being, entering into our condition, and judges us not from above but from alongside us. It may be that John is also thinking of the powerful figure of the son of man mentioned in Daniel 7:13–14, who comes from heaven and is given 'authority, glory and sovereign power' over all nations.

He was ensnared in rejection (vv. 31–47). The responsibilities Jesus shoulders mean that he shares not only in the joys and authority of the Father, but in his heartache and rejection too. He faces that rejection in spite of many witnesses who speak up in his defence. The idea of a trial runs through the Gospel,[23] and here it is as if Jesus is calling witness after witness to testify to the truth of his claims and the validity of his actions. He calls on John the Baptist (vv. 33–34), but people took notice of him only briefly and had misgivings about him as soon as his celebrity status began to wane. As his next witness, he calls on the works he has done (v. 36), but people argued that they were unconvincing. Then he calls on the scriptures

(vv. 37–39), where God himself had spoken and pointed to his coming, but, in spite of much study, people failed to see Jesus in them. He then even goes back to Moses (vv. 45–47), the great founder of Israel who prophesied that one day a prophet like himself would come and speak the words of God (Deuteronomy 18:17–19), but they do not even pay any attention to him. So, Jesus warns them, Moses will serve not only as a witness in his defence but an accuser in their prosecution.

How sad that people in Jesus' day went after all sorts of deluded leaders who set themselves up as gurus and followed sometimes the most abusive of teachers, as they still do! So often they seemed determined not to listen to the one who was the teacher of truth and bringer of life. And just as they had rejected his Father, so they would reject him, ultimately by nailing him to a cross.

The glory of the Son is intimately bound up with the glory of the Father. It is, wrote Michael Ramsey, 'in the dependence and submission of the Son throughout his earthly mission, that the deepest meaning of glory lies'.[24] The Father's glory is seen in the life of the Son, and the vocation of the Son is to glorify the Father.

Questions

1. This passage reports the way in which the Jewish leaders called into question the authority of Jesus. What authority do you grant Jesus and his teaching in your own life?

2. Jesus refused to accept glory (honour or approval) from human beings (v. 41). Where do we look for approval and what are the sources from which we derive affirmation? Are they human or divine?

11

The glory of the abundant provider

JOHN 6:1–15, 25–59

The glory of Jesus was observed in what he did and what he said. Seven miraculous signs punctuate John's Gospel. So too do seven claims that Jesus makes about himself, each beginning with the significant words, 'I am…' The signs and the sayings first flow together in chapter 6. Here we have the fourth sign (the feeding of the five thousand) and the first saying: 'I am the bread of life'. In bringing them together like this, Jesus gives astonishing proof that his claim is not an empty one. It is as if he is providing his audience with a free sample of an offer that he will one day make to all.

At this stage, the popularity of Jesus was continuing to grow, in spite of (or perhaps because of) the opposition of the Jewish leaders. But popularity has its price. It meant that Jesus could get little rest, even when he went to the far shore of Lake Galilee, for the crowds followed him everywhere. What do you do with all these crowds? Who provides for their practical needs? If they are following you, perhaps you will be held responsible. It was on one such occasion that Jesus gave a practical demonstration of his claim to be 'the bread of life'.

Practical demonstration (vv. 1–14)

It was *a necessary provision*. After hours of travelling, followed perhaps by hours of listening, the 5000-strong crowd would have been weary and hungry. Unless they were fed, they might become restive. A riot might even be provoked. So when Jesus stepped in, it was not to dazzle them with sensational luxuries but to supply them with what was essential. John Calvin pointed out that 'of his own accord Christ takes care of those who neglect themselves' in order to follow him. Christ does not wait until they are starving and crying out for food because they have nothing to eat, since he provides food for them even before they ask for it.[25]

It was also *a miraculous provision*. When Jesus confronted Philip with the problem, he already knew the solution. Philip could only respond in despair. Feeding such a crowd would swallow up two-thirds of an annual wage, he replied, and even then the people would have no more than a bite each. When you think of it, the situation was pretty hopeless. There were no mobile caterers around, and if there were any villages nearby, they wouldn't have been able to cope with such an influx of unexpected visitors, even if someone could have footed the bill.

At this point, Andrew introduces a lad to Jesus who has brought lunch with him, although it is unclear why he does so. It was only a couple of fish and a few coarse loaves, but maybe Andrew really believed that Jesus could make use of it. He seems to spoil it, however, when he adds, 'But how far will they go among so many?' Whatever brief moment of faith he had seems quickly to evaporate.

The mention of 'barley loaves' indicates that this boy was not from a wealthy family, for barley loaves were what the poor ate. Maybe John tells us this detail for another reason as well. Elisha once miraculously fed a whole crowd with a few barley loaves (2 Kings 4:42–44). Can Jesus do the same? Is he a prophet of equal standing? Jesus takes the offering, gives thanks for it and then multiplies it as it is served to the waiting crowd.

It was *an abundant provision*. Jesus passes the test with flying colours. When everyone had eaten their fill, the disciples were sent by Jesus to clean up the mess and gather the scraps of food left over. When they did so, they found that they had twelve baskets full. In other words, they ended up with far more than they had at first.

Jesus was demonstrating the generosity of God's provision and the abundance of his power once more, just as he had done when he turned water into wine at Cana.

Scriptural foundation (vv. 31–33, 49–50, 58)

The physical act was intended to demonstrate a spiritual truth. It was a window on to something much larger than the provision of one day's lunch, however big the crowd. Here, surely, was a revelation of God's majestic power. Who could avoid the comparison to a remarkably similar act of God that had taken place previously in a wilderness, when the children of Israel complained about hunger? Exodus 16 records that God provided for them by raining down bread from heaven. They spoke of it as an appearance of God's glory.

The rabbis believed that when the Messiah came, he would produce manna from heaven. They are not impressed with the bread that Jesus has provided and try to compare his work poorly with that of Moses. But Jesus will have none of it. Moses was not the source of the manna: God was. Those who ate that manna in the wilderness still died. The bread that Jesus provides also comes from heaven, but those who eat it will never die. Furthermore, his provision is not limited to one people. His bread 'gives life to the world'. The bread that Jesus offers is altogether superior.

Just as the children of Israel saw the glory of God in the provision of manna in the wilderness, so now the Messiah has come and his glory is seen once again in the miraculous provision of food in a desert place.

Personal revelation (vv. 14–58)

The sensation-seeking crowd called Jesus a prophet and wanted to make him king, simply because they were enjoying the spectacle of his miracles. The more he did, the more they wanted, but they really had no intention of letting him reign over them. They wanted him as a puppet-king, who could satisfy their every whim. They weren't prepared to adopt the sort of kingship he wanted to exercise.

The discussion about how many miracles they want Jesus to perform leads him to reveal his hand. Explaining what he has just done, he tells them straight that he is 'the bread of life'. Their persistent questioning leads him to state more than once that he is the true bread from heaven. If they are to enjoy eternal life, he is the bread they should be eating. In J.B. Lightfoot's words, 'He does not merely impart a gift which He brings; He is that gift.'[26]

Enduring application (vv. 27, 29, 51–59)

The image of Jesus as the bread of life has contemporary significance.

First, it reminds us to *eat the right food* (v. 27). Our diet has recently become a matter of widespread public concern. We are consuming so much junk and processed food that we are facing a major health crisis, especially with the rise in heart conditions and obesity. As it is physically, so it is spiritually. We need to feed our spirits on the right food if we are to enjoy spiritual health and, especially, if we are to enjoy eternal life. The 'food' that so many people work for is like junk food: it does no good in the long term. Money, fame, status, reputation, pleasure and even education are inadequate fare with which to sustain a good life. None of these things deal in the currency of heaven. Calvin says that Jesus knew people were 'bound by earthly cares' and needed to be set free from them before 'they may arise to heaven'.[27] As it was then, so, even more, is it now.

Second, it reminds us to *believe the right person* (v. 29). The Jews seemed keen to win God's approval and wanted to know what they could do to serve him. Typically, they were thinking of what they could do for God, as if he was dependent on them in some way.

Jesus tells them that it is not their works but their faith that matters: 'The work of God is this: to believe in the one he has sent.' It is whether you trust and follow Jesus, not how busy you are in good deeds, that makes the difference.

Third, it reminds us to *adopt the right approach* (vv. 51–56). A host may spend time preparing the most wonderful gourmet meal but it is wasted unless the guests sit down at the table and eat it. Jesus invited people to eat the life-sustaining bread that God had provided from heaven. Admiration was not enough. Consumption was essential. But perhaps it is not surprising that people were puzzled. Since Jesus is the bread from heaven, he tells them that they have to eat his flesh and drink his blood. It's not cannibalism he has in mind, as later critics of Christianity suspected. What he means is this: we derive life from the food we inwardly digest; so we will derive life from Christ if, by faith, we absorb him into the innermost aspects of our lives. Occasional, superficial, outward acknowledgment of Christ is not enough. He must become part of us.

As in the days of Moses and Elisha, so now in the days of Jesus the Messiah, bread is provided for a hungry people and the glory of God is seen again in his abundant provision.

Questions

1. If you had been among the hungry crowd that day, what would you have made of the event?

2. The Lord's Prayer teaches us to pray for daily bread and ends by proclaiming God's kingdom, power and glory. How far do we see the daily provision of food as a sign of God's glory?

12

The glory of the creation's master

JOHN 6:16–24

The illusionist David Blaine was in the headlines in late October 2003. He had just completed his latest stunt, which consisted of fasting for 44 days while suspended high in the air in a glass box near Tower Bridge in London. He emerged thinner but relatively healthy. Some people were full of admiration. Some thought he was crazy. Perhaps even more, given his profession, thought he had deceived them. It was all, they said, trickery.

It is amazing how the report of Jesus walking on water provokes this last reaction. People find it unbelievable and assume that Jesus was an illusionist. Several explanations are offered to debunk it. He must have been walking on the shore and, in the darkness, his disciples just thought he was walking on the water. He never left the shallows and the disciples didn't see his feet sink below the surface of the water. The most incredulous of all suggest that he walked out to them on carefully placed stepping-stones! But these rationalizations won't work. They just don't fit the facts.

Matthew and Mark also tell this story (Matthew 14:22–36; Mark 6:45–52). That's unusual because most of John's miracles are not mentioned in the other Gospels. Their accounts support John's while giving a few extra details. They all tell us that it happened after the feeding of the five thousand (the only other miracle they all record). They agree that it happened at night, with Matthew adding that it was in the early hours of the morning. They all say that the disciples were in difficulty, battling against the stormy wind. They all agree that Jesus walked out to them, 'walking on the water'. They all report that when the disciples saw it, they were, understandably, terrified. They all agree, too, that when Jesus saw their reaction, he told them, as he often did in unusual circumstances, not to be afraid.

In spite of all that agreement, each Gospel writer ends the story somewhat differently. Mark is content to report that the wind died down. Matthew tells us that, too, but adds the famous account of Peter trying to walk on water. John says that they had managed to row only three and a half miles before Jesus appeared, which puts them roughly in the middle of the lake. (That's why the silly suggestions that he was walking on the shore or in the shallows just won't do.) When Jesus came to them, however, 'immediately the boat reached the shore where they were heading'. The remaining four miles or so seem to have been completed instantly.

So much for the story, but what does it mean? How does it display the glory of God in Jesus? The glory of Jesus erupts from this short story like a starburst.

We see the glory of the Lord of creation

Walking on water violates the laws of nature. It can't be done. Water will not sustain the weight of a human body. We may float in a swimming pool or even in the Dead Sea, but we can't walk three and a half miles across a deep and stormy lake. The phrase has come to mean doing something that is impossible. So how did Jesus do it? The Bible doesn't tell us. 'How?' is a modern question, typical of a Western mindset. Knowing 'how' sometimes prevents someone from looking deeper and asking 'why?'—the question that the Bible is more concerned about.

Jesus walked on water because he was the Lord of creation, not subject to its laws. Rather, they were subject to him. The great claims made about his role in bringing planet earth into being— claims found in John 1, Colossians 1 and Hebrews 1—find their outworking here. If he made it, sustains it, upholds it and rules it, then he can walk on water.

We see the glory of the Master of evil powers

The Sea of Galilee was well known for its sudden storms, caused by its position in the Jordan valley, with high mountains to the east and west. The cool air would rush down from the mountain heights with great force, causing tempestuous eruptions on the lake. Even today, Galilean fishermen call the early evening easterly wind *Sharkia*, which is Arabic for 'shark'. The Jews had long viewed the sea with some degree of fear, believing that it was the abode of the forces of Leviathan and other monsters who sought to bring chaos to people's lives (see Job 3:8; 41:1; Isaiah 27:1). The storms experienced by the disciples as they crossed the Sea of Galilee would have only reinforced their anxieties. The sea was a dwelling place for evil powers that threatened destruction.

Psalm 74:12–14 celebrates the defeat of chaos by God the king. Malevolent forces would wreak havoc, but they prove impotent in the face of God's beneficial and majestic rule. When Jesus walked on water, he was conquering the destructive forces of the deep, banishing them into helplessness and demonstrating his sovereign power—a power just like God's—over all.

We see the glory of the Saviour of drowning people

We must never lose sight of the fact that real people were caught in the midst of this spiritual skirmish. Although they might have been experienced fishermen, their lives were endangered and they were terrified. At one time I was the chaplain to a lifeboat crew. They were hardened men who had clocked up many a courageous rescue in the most dangerous of conditions, but they knew their limitations in comparison with the sea, and their reactions to it ranged from nothing less than healthy respect to, on occasions, outright terror.

When Jesus came to his disciples across the water, he not only defeated their enemies and stilled the storm but brought them safely, and quickly, to the shore. They experienced, in a real sense, his salvation.

When the early Church read this story and the other one like it, where Jesus falls asleep on a boat in the middle of a furious storm (Mark 4:35–41), they took it as a symbol of the way Jesus dealt not only with the meteorological storms that his disciples encountered but also with the other kinds of storms that blow in life. William Barclay writes that 'it is a sign and the symbol of what he always does for his people, when the wind is contrary and when we are in danger of being overwhelmed by the storms of life'.[28] Augustine put it even more succinctly: 'He came treading the waves and so he puts all the tumults of life under his feet. Christians, why be afraid?'[29]

We see the glory of the incarnate Son of God

What Jesus did on the day he walked on water echoes two Old Testament texts that speak of God striding through the sea. Psalm 77:16, 19 says, 'The waters saw you, O God, the waters saw you and writhed; the very depths were convulsed... Your path led through the sea, your way through the mighty waters, though your footprints were not seen.' Job 9:8 says that God 'alone stretches out the heavens and treads on the waves of the sea'. The former passage speaks of the God of the exodus, who sets his people free from forces that oppress them. The latter speaks of God's unquestioned sovereignty over the creation he has made.

When he walked on water, Jesus brought both those texts to life. He showed himself to be God incarnate, still saving and still sovereign.

George Beasley-Murray helpfully pointed out that 'the account would be unbelievable in relation to anyone else, but in Jesus we are dealing with the one who in his humanity was in a unique relation to God, the incarnate Son of God, in the process of inaugurating the kingdom of God through his living and dying and rising. If no one else in history has walked on water, neither has any other human being had that origin, that calling, and that destiny'.[30] Quite so.

Walking on water was no illusion. It was the right of the unique Son of God to do so. It was a further revelation of his glory, which was seen in his Lordship over creation, his mastery of evil powers, and his rescuing of the drowning fishermen.

Questions

1. After the feeding of the five thousand, the crowds wanted to make Jesus king by force (John 6:15). He refused to play their game. Why? And how does walking on the water demonstrate his sovereign kingship?

2. Why are people so keen to explain this miracle away? How much does it matter to you if this miracle did not take place but is no more than a nice story?

13

The glory of the flowing stream

JOHN 7:1–52

It was one of our family's most embarrassing experiences and I was responsible. We had borrowed a friend's cottage in an isolated spot in the country for a holiday with another family. We'd had a great time. On our final evening, we got the kids ready for their baths. We turned on the water and, after an angry splutter, behold, no water. The owner had warned me! Whether it rains or not, he said, check the inlet to the tank which is situated a couple of fields up the hill and supplies the water to the house every day. It had rained plenty during the holiday. I hadn't listened to the owner and as a result the tank had run dry. A massive air lock had occurred and the result was that they had to dig up a field and vent the system to get it working again.

Water is one of those things that we take for granted, until we don't have it. They never took it for granted in Israel. That's why it served as a powerful metaphor throughout the Bible, and that's why Jesus spoke of it to reveal a further facet of his glory.

Jesus was biding his time. At first he did not go up to celebrate the feast of Tabernacles in Jerusalem with his sceptical brothers because they were pushing him to publicize himself, as if he were a worldly politician standing for election. When, halfway through the feast, he did go up, he went on his own terms, not theirs. Jesus immediately became the centre of attention with his controversial teaching. The really interesting thing, though, happened right at the end of the feast.

The ceremony he transforms (vv. 1–7, 37–39)

Israel was hot and dry. Much of it was desert, created by the scorching heat of the sun and relieved only by the occasional lush oasis, like the land around the city of Jericho. The lack of water was a perpetual threat to the growth of crops and the abundance of harvests. Underground springs were treated as a precious resource and careful irrigation techniques were developed to water the fields. But life in Israel was precarious; people lived in the face of constant uncertainty.

The need for water was etched deep into the nation's psyche. That was why the prophets spoke so frequently about a dry and thirsty land and also why they used the imagery of springs and watered land as a symbol of prosperity and God's blessing.

This need for water was captured in a particular ritual that took place each year in the third week in October, during the annual feast of Tabernacles. Usually the most popular of the Jewish feasts, it was attended by massive crowds and brought the annual round of festivals to a conclusion, celebrating the gathering in of the grape and olive harvests. It got its name from the flimsy constructions that pilgrims erected out of palm branches for their temporary accommodation.

Each day during the feast, the Jews collected water from the pool of Siloam in a golden vessel and paraded it through the streets to the temple. When they got to the Water Gate, there were three blasts from a ceremonial ram's horn, and the verse Isaiah 12:3—'With joy you will draw water from the wells of salvation'—was declared to the crowds. The water was brought to the high priest while the choir sang the Psalms of thanksgiving and praise (Psalms 113—118). Every male pilgrim joined in the climax, waving citrus fruit and branches in the air and crying, 'Give thanks to the Lord!' three times as the water was poured out as an offering to God.

It is unclear whether this ceremony took place on the 'last and greatest day of the Feast' (v. 37). Whether it did or not, it is clear that

Jesus tops it as he proclaims that he is the source of never-failing water and that he can satisfy the need of the thirstiest person.

The vision he fulfils

As the Jews looked to their future, they prayed for the coming of a Messiah who would free them from their enemies and bring in a new age of prosperity and peace. One of the key symbols of that age, on which they focused many hopes, was that water would at last be in plentiful supply. They looked back to the way God had miraculously supplied water from a rock when their ancestors were in the wilderness (the story is found in Exodus 17:1–7 and Numbers 20:1–13) and they longed for him to do it again, only this time in perpetuity.

The prophets regularly took up the same theme. One example is found in Isaiah 44:3, but the most important prophecies about it occur in Ezekiel 47:1–12, where the prophet pictures water flowing from the heart of the temple, getting deeper and deeper until it becomes a huge river beside which vegetation flourishes and within which fish swarm. Zechariah 14:8 similarly foretold how 'on that day [the day of the Messiah] living water will flow out from Jerusalem, half to the eastern sea and half to the western sea, in summer and in winter'. In both visions, the source of water was found in the temple, the centre of Jerusalem. If we were able to ask the prophets to locate it more precisely, they might well have replied that it flowed from the rock on which the temple stood. In other words, God would do again what he had done in the desert. Life-giving water would flow from a rock once more.

When Jesus stood in the Jerusalem temple and proclaimed that he could satisfy the needs of the thirstiest, he was saying that all these prophecies were finding their fulfilment in him. So, too, were all the aspirations of the feast of Tabernacles. What the feast itself could not deliver, he could. He fine-tunes those hopes somewhat and adds that 'whoever believes in me… will have streams of living water flowing from within'. These words can be read, in the original, more than one way. Contrary to many standard translations, he is probably not saying that all who believe in him will have streams of living water flowing within *them*. This would mean that their lives were not only constantly resourced but a source of continuous refreshment for others. While that may be true, he is more probably saying that the streams of living water flow from deep within *him* into the lives of believers. The streams do not become the possession of believers. Jesus is the one and only source of water, and believers remain totally dependent on him as the perpetual source of refreshment, cleansing and transformation.

John goes on to explain more fully what Jesus meant. The stream stood for the Holy Spirit, whose coming, when Jesus spoke, still lay in the future. The Spirit was, and is, never anything other than the Spirit of Jesus. He does not operate independently of Jesus, but continues his work of cleansing, transforming, refreshing and enabling fruitfulness to grow in the lives of Jesus' followers.

The invitation he offers (vv. 39–37)

Jesus was doing more than making a statement; he was issuing an invitation. Those who were thirsty, whose lives were barren and who were running on empty, were welcome to come to him and have their thirst quenched. In making the offer, he made use of the very words that God had spoken in Isaiah 55:1 when he invited any who were spiritually dry to return to him and find refreshment, provided freely out of his grace. Once more, Jesus was putting himself on a par with God. This was clearly no empty boast, however, because the woman from Samaria, whom we met in chapter 4, was a living demonstration of the genuineness of his invitation.

Like all invitations, though, it is worthless unless we accept it and avail ourselves of the offer.

The reaction he provokes (vv. 40–52)

In the rest of this chapter, John keeps us informed of public opinion about Jesus, which was very mixed. His brothers displayed half-amused contempt. Many in the crowd displayed open curiosity. Others were intellectually dismissive. They knew their scriptures, or so they thought, and wrote him off on the basis of a half-truth that they believed, about the Messiah coming from Bethlehem. The leaders and officials reacted with ill-disguised hatred, but some refused to dismiss him too quickly. Their verdict was that by doing what he did and saying what he said, he must be showing himself to be 'the Prophet'. Some even went further and courageously identified him as 'the Christ', the expected Messiah.

The question of who Jesus was assumes a growing importance in the rest of John's Gospel. What he said in the temple on 'the last and greatest day of the Feast' gave them a further glimpse of his glory and an insight into his mission. From him flows a stream of living water, teeming, vibrant, invigorating, reviving, refreshing, bubbling, life-giving, thirst-quenching, fruit-bearing and transforming. And the stream is in permanent flow. It will never run dry.

Questions

1. Like the miracle of walking on water, Jesus' invitation to the thirsty connects his mission with the renewal of creation. Look at Romans 8:20–21, 1 Corinthians 15, Colossians 1:20 and 2 Peter 3:13. How broad is your vision of the future? Do you share the hope not only of personally entering 'heaven' but also of seeing our broken creation restored to wholeness through the work of Jesus?

2. Meditate on Isaiah 35:1–2 and 41:17–19. Are you in need of the refreshing ministry of the Holy Spirit today?

14

The glory of the shining light

JOHN 8:12–59

Glory and light somehow belong together. Glory suggests splendour, radiance, brilliance, effulgence, incandescence. So perhaps it should be no surprise that Jesus, in whom they saw glory, announces that he is 'the light of the world'. Initially, this claim—the second of his 'I am' sayings—seems to stand in isolation, as if on an island surrounded by a sea of controversy. The nearest shore on one side contains a few introductory comments about the light having come into the world, but that is as far back as chapters 1 and 3 and little was made of the claim there. The nearest shore on the other side looks to be in chapter 9, where the claim is validated as a blind man is made to see. But if that miracle is meant to be the sign that backs up Jesus' claim to be 'the light of the world', there is a long argument in between that gets in the way.

The claim is not isolated, however. The argument that follows it in chapter 8 is not irrelevant but essential to our understanding. It helps us grasp the darkness that Jesus came to dispel. Why was it that Jesus chose the image of light to speak about his mission?

The light he radiates

As with much of Jesus' teaching, he is not creating a new image out of his own fertile imagination. He is drawing on the deep roots of the Old Testament to show how those roots are bearing fruit at last, now that he has come. The image of light was used in at least three different ways in the ancient scriptures.

First, light was associated with *the creation of life*. According to Genesis 1:1–3, God's first step in creating the world was to overcome darkness, create light and separate day (light) from night (darkness). When he saw the results, he pronounced them 'good'. Light provides the conditions in which life can begin. It is an essential requirement for life. Without it, life remains dormant. Kent's Cavern is a complex of prehistoric caves that prove popular with holidaymakers who visit Torquay, on the south Devon coast in the UK. All sorts of seeds lay dormant in them for centuries, until electric light was installed for the convenience of the tourists. Then a multitude of prehistoric ferns sprang into life. God's light is even more necessary than physical light if human beings are to enjoy life to the full.

Second, light was associated with *the giving of direction*. Psalm 119:105 says, 'Your word is a lamp to my feet and a light for my path'. The rabbis talked of the law as illuminating the way ahead so that wise choices could be made, and pitfalls and stumbling blocks avoided. God's word serves sometimes as a lighthouse warning us of danger, sometimes as a searchlight picking out a difficult path, sometimes as a street light guiding us through the ordinary walkways of life and sometimes even as a dim torch, keeping hope alive when darkness would otherwise extinguish it.

Third, light was associated with *the mission of Israel*. Israel was commissioned, according to Isaiah 42:6–7, to bring light to the Gentiles. The privileges of salvation and of walking in the light of God's truth that Israel had experienced were not to be kept to themselves. They had a mission to share those privileges with pagan nations. They were 'to open eyes that are blind, to free captives from prison, and to release from the dungeon those who sit in darkness'. What Israel failed to do because of its narrow nationalism and introverted piety, Jesus, the Messiah, now took upon himself to do. He was to be the light, not of the Jews alone, but 'of the world'.

In claiming to be the light of the world, Jesus was claiming to give life, provide direction, reveal truth and embrace the whole world in the glory of God's liberating grace.

The darkness he encounters

No sooner has Jesus made this great claim than he is mired in controversy with the Jewish leaders again. It seems something of an anticlimax. The plot unfolds this way intentionally rather than accidentally, however. John is telling us that as soon as the claim is made, the light-bringer encounters the very darkness he has come to dispel. It was not the darkness of physical blindness or of the absence of physical light, but it was a real darkness even so. It was the darkness of religious prejudice and spiritual arrogance that expressed itself in a number of ways.

First, there was *the darkness of ignorance* (vv. 13–30). We speak of people who do not know a piece of news as being 'in the dark'. The Pharisees whom Jesus encountered were certainly that. They had an extremely limited worldview and could only evaluate things 'by human standards'. There was so much they were missing. They didn't have the full picture, and they certainly couldn't see things from God's viewpoint. So, when it came to Jesus, they persistently misunderstood him. They thought he was blowing his own trumpet (v. 13), speaking of his human rather than his heavenly father (v. 19) and threatening suicide when he was predicting his crucifixion (v. 22), and they were mystified about his identity (v. 25). Yet Jesus came so that, through being 'lifted up', he could show people who he really was and, by dying for them, put them back in touch with his Father. He came to dispel ignorance and give people the full picture.

Second, there was *the darkness of slavery* (vv. 31–37). No human being should have to suffer the indignity of slavery. It is an evil that enlightened politicians have done much to eliminate over the centuries. For the Jews, it was the worst form of indignity possible, since God had made them to be free. Yet Jesus accuses these respectable leaders of Israel of being in bondage, not to Rome but to sin. Sin is a potent force and, once given a foothold, soon asserts its authority over us and subjects us to servitude. Highlighting one aspect of slavery, Jesus points out that being a slave is a very different experience from being a son. Sons belong in the family permanently. Slaves never 'belong' nor enjoy security in their relationships. But Jesus came to release people from slavery to sin—and other forms of bondage as well—and does so by revealing his truth. As people follow this truth, they walk his well-lit road to freedom.

Third, there was *the darkness of deception* (vv. 38–47). The mention of 'family' means that the conversation turns to family trees. The Pharisees boast of having Abraham as their patriarch, but Jesus says that their actions show them to belong to a rather different family line altogether. Their desire to kill him, their refusal to accept his truth and their addiction to lies demonstrate that their real father is the devil. He has lying and murder in his genes, and his deceptive tactics have seduced the Pharisees into thinking that if they oppose Jesus they are doing God's will. Not so! Jesus came to expose Satan's deceptions and give people the opportunity to live by the truth.

Fourth, there was *the darkness of hatred* (v. 59). The Jews' murderous intent increases in intensity throughout the conversation. The episode ends with them picking up stones, ready to do away with Jesus. Hatred, suspicion, mistrust, fear and arrogance run like evil threads through all that they say and do. They boil over when Jesus puts himself in a position that is superior to Abraham's. Ironically, his purpose in coming was to banish hatred and to lead people to experience love—love from God—and to reproduce it in their relationships with others.

One of Graham Kendrick's songs sums it up:

> *Darkness like a shroud*
> *covers the earth,*
> *evil like a cloud*
> *covers the people;*

but the Lord will rise upon you,
and His glory will appear on you,
nations will come to your light.

Arise, shine, your light has come,
the glory of the Lord has risen on you;
arise, shine, your light has come—
Jesus the light of the world has come.

'ARISE, SHINE' BY GRAHAM KENDRICK. COPYRIGHT © 1985 THANKYOUMUSIC

In his claim to be the light of the world, the Pharisees thought that Jesus was being absurdly arrogant and 'seeking glory for himself'. That was their fundamental mistake. It was really God, the one whom they claimed to know and serve, who was glorifying him (vv. 50–54). God held him in high honour and was shining the brilliant rays of his light into the world through Jesus.

The light that Jesus radiates sheds knowledge where there is ignorance, freedom where there is bondage, truth where there are lies and love where there is hatred. Since the darkness is still palpable in our world, we can only pray, 'Shine, Jesus, shine.'

Questions

1. How far do you look to the Bible as a source of guidance to spread light on your path? Or do you neglect it, looking elsewhere for direction in life?

2. Think of any situations of darkness that you know of today. Is it possible for you to shed the light of Jesus into any of those situations and so fulfil the mission that Israel neglected?

15

The glory of the divine luminary

JOHN 9:1–41

Jesus' claim to be the light of the world is put to the test in an encounter with one solitary man. We do not know his name. We only know that he was blind from birth and that by the time he met Jesus he was an adult. When the Israelites were commissioned to be a light to the Gentiles, they were expected to go and 'open eyes that are blind' (Isaiah 42:7). Would Jesus succeed where they had failed? Would he prove able to bring light into the darkness of this man's life?

The action Jesus took (vv. 1–7)

Chapter 9 opens with a false assumption, a true purpose and a strange action.

The disciples, who saw the man and assumed that his blindness had been caused by sin, voice the *false assumption*. They may not have commented on the matter, except that somehow they knew he been born without sight. Perhaps he was a well-known figure whose begging for alms meant that they had heard his story before. As religious Jews, they would have taken it for granted that such suffering was a punishment for wrongdoing but, since he had been born that way, a question arose: who had committed the sin? The man himself could not be to blame, so was it his parents? Jesus disabuses them of the notion that there is always a direct causal connection between suffering and sin. There may be, as the story of the healing at the pool of Bethesda suggests, but it is not always so.

Jesus suggests that, in this case, the *true purpose* for his suffering was 'so that the work of God might be displayed in his life' (v. 3). Jesus obviously knew that he was about to give the man his sight. Yet this was not just another miracle. It was a miracle that would either support or undermine Jesus' claim to be 'the light of the world'. If he could bring light into the darkness of this man's life, the claim would be borne out. If not, it would remain highly questionable, even if not actually refuted.

Reflecting on this, William Temple commented that 'the vitally important question is not "Who is responsible?"—*this man or his parents*—but "How can this fact be turned to the glory of God?"' Temple continued, somewhat robustly, 'All things exist for that glory; even sin and every form of evil, is compelled to minister to that glory; and the opportunity of glorifying God is the ultimate factor in every situation.'[31]

So Jesus sets to work. His method on this occasion involves *a strange action*. He makes some eye-salve from a mixture of the dust on the ground and his own spittle and anoints the blind man's eyes. Quite why he chose to do this is uncertain. The Gospels do not usually show a concern with the mechanics of the miracles they report. It could be that the use of the dust was a reminder of God creating Adam from the dust of the earth (Genesis 2:7) and a symbol that a new creation was about to take place. Or it could be that Jesus was using saliva because, in the ancient world, many people thought it contained healing properties: we know that other 'healers' used it. Also, the command to wash in the pool of Siloam echoes the command to Naaman to wash in the Jordan so that he might be healed (2 Kings 5). Perhaps these were all ways of aiding the blind man's faith. Although we cannot be sure what was in Jesus' mind, there is one thing of which we can be sure: the man was blind but, after Jesus took action, he could see. The restoration of his sight was an irrefutable, if inexplicable, fact.

The confession Jesus provoked (vv. 8–38)

The miracle is followed by an extraordinary game of cat-and-mouse, with the blind man playing the part of the mouse. First, his neighbours doubt him, thinking that it's a look-alike who has been healed. They can't believe it is the same man. Then, the Pharisees quiz him, refusing to accept that Jesus could have healed him. Next, his parents abandon him, fearing the consequences of getting involved. 'He's old enough,' they say, 'to speak for himself.' After that, the Pharisees interrogate him again, turning the screw, insisting that the man must be in league with Jesus, and end up by throwing him out of the temple as a sinner. Finally, Jesus re-enters the story and explains more fully the meaning of all that has been going on.

The account reads humorously, although it must have been stressful for the poor man at the time. The more the Pharisees try to deny the miracle, the more adamant the man becomes that it happened. And the more they try to blacken Jesus' character, the more the man is persuaded that Jesus is more than ordinary. He takes his stand on the straightforward fact that 'I was blind but now I see'. This fact is stated five times in these encounters, one way or another, and each time the newly sighted man is pushed to take the logic of his healing a little further—in exactly the opposite direction to the way the Pharisees want him to move in his thinking.

He starts by saying that he knows nothing personally of the miracle worker but has heard that the man's name was Jesus. When he says this, in verse 11, he implies that he has no reason to think that Jesus is anything other than an ordinary man. There were many miracle workers in the ancient world and they didn't all claim divinity simply because they could do a few healings. But since the religious authorities are making all this fuss about Jesus, he begins to think that he must be a prophet (v. 17). When the opposition really gets going and they denounce Jesus as a sinner, he knows that their logic doesn't add up. So next he exposes the absurd inner contradictions of their arguments and concludes that, since God had heard Jesus' prayer and granted the healing, he must be a man from God (v. 33).

The climax of his logic, and his confession, do not come, however, when he is being quizzed by the Pharisees but only when he meets up with Jesus once more (vv. 35–38). Jesus speaks of himself as 'the Son of Man'—the powerful figure described in Daniel 7 who comes to earth from God to establish God's kingdom and exercise his judgment. The man knows that there is only one response possible in the presence of such a person: that is, to bow in worship and kneel in trust.

The meaning Jesus gave (vv. 39–41)

Jesus explains the deeper meaning of what's been happening. His miracle was a sign of a deeper truth—an acted parable, which used the physical to illustrate the spiritual. The people who are really blind, Jesus says, are those who think they can see the things of God clearly when, in fact, their sight is so impaired that they cannot even recognize Jesus as the Son of Man. It doesn't take the religious leaders long to realize that he is talking about them. Their lack of vision, Jesus says, is culpable and leads to judgment. But the people whom those very leaders accused of being blind were the ones who often exercised faith and who really could see.

Here, then, is another sign of Jesus' glory: a miracle that reveals that his claim to be the light of the world is far from empty. William Barclay wrote:

The other Gospels stress the compassion of the miracles; the Fourth Gospel stresses the fact that the miracles are manifestations of power and glory. Surely there is no real contradiction here. It is simply two ways of looking at the same thing. And at the heart of it there is the supreme truth that the glory of God lies in His compassion, and that God never so fully reveals His glory as when He reveals His pity.[32]

This sign is about the triumph of light over darkness. It reveals the glory of the divine luminary. He who lit the cosmos as he flung the sun and the stars into space, and he who enlightens the world with his love and his truth, is also the one who can bring light into the life of one blind individual and cause him to see. The luminous majesty of God is manifest in it all.

Questions

1. Consider the various ways in which Jesus is described in this passage: the man called Jesus, sinner, prophet, Christ, Son of Man (for Son of Man in v. 35, see Daniel 7:13–14). What do these names mean? Which describes Jesus most adequately to you and why?

2. Our society considers physical blindness a severe disability, but how do we view spiritual blindness? Do we treat it less seriously?

16

The glory of the good shepherd

JOHN 10:1–21

Urban Westerners have a quite sentimental view of the shepherd, aided and abetted by feeble Sunday school pictures that portray Jesus in a quite unbiblical way as a gentle shepherd, 'meek and mild', cuddling fleecy lambs. The truth is that being a shepherd in ancient times was an arduous and dangerous job, an occupation for roughnecks rather than more refined individuals. Alastair Campbell captures it well when he compares the life of a shepherd to that of a cowboy in the Wild West rather than the gentle-mannered pastors and bishops who often come to mind.[33] Indeed, in the time of Jesus, shepherding was on a list of despised occupations. Shepherds lived on the margins of normal society—the demands of the job meant that they couldn't lead a predictable, stable life. So they were usually ritually unclean as far as temple worship was concerned, and were routinely considered dishonest as far as anything else was concerned. It is startling, then, that Jesus presents himself as 'the good shepherd'. There wasn't likely to be much glory in that. Why did he do so?

The false shepherds of Israel

Living in a rural economy, the image of the shepherd naturally suggested itself to the Israelites as a metaphor for leadership, and the symbol became widely used for prophets, priests and kings.

Leaders were to guide, provide, defend, discipline and nurse their people, just as shepherds did with the flocks for which they were responsible. The problem was that the leader-shepherds of Israel regularly failed in their duties. They used their sheep to their own ends, living *off* them rather than *for* them. They often behaved more like butchers than shepherds. Prophets preached false prophecies rather than true words from the Lord. Priests offered blemished sacrifices rather than the pure sacrifices of those with clean hands and pure hearts. Kings ruled with selfish intent rather than with compassionate justice.

This led the true spokesmen of God to condemn the leaders of Israel as false shepherds who had neglected their calling and abdicated their responsibilities. Ezekiel 34 contains one such denunciation and Zechariah 11:4–17 another. The former condemned them as 'only taking care of themselves' (v. 2), while the latter condemned them as worthless shepherds who ate 'the meat of the choice sheep, tearing off their hoofs' and left the rest of the defenceless flock to scatter and perish.

Ezekiel's prophecy contains not only doom but also hope, however. God goes on to say that where the leaders have failed, he will step in and be the shepherd of Israel himself. Unable to trust others, he will assume direct responsibility for his injured and frightened flock. 'I myself will search for my sheep and look after them… I will rescue them… I will bring them out… I will pasture them… I will tend them… I will search for the lost and bring back the strays. I will bind up the injured and strengthen the weak… I will shepherd the flock with justice' (Ezekiel 34:11–16).

The true shepherd of Israel

When Jesus declared himself to be 'the good shepherd', he was claiming for himself the promise of Ezekiel. What Ezekiel had prophesied was being accomplished through his coming.

The picture Jesus paints is complex. Initially, he speaks of being the shepherd; before long, he is speaking about being the gate. But even if the image is fluid, the meaning is crystal clear. He is spelling out what makes him the good shepherd.

First, there is *his intimate knowledge of his sheep* (v. 3). To the inexpert eye, one sheep looks pretty much like another. The fraudulent shepherd wouldn't care even if they were individuals. A genuine shepherd, on the other hand, knows his sheep well enough to enjoy their distinct features and personalities and will mark them out by giving them names. The names may well be humorous, picking up on some lovable (or annoying) quality that distinguishes one from another. But they are names nonetheless and, if they are used often enough, the sheep will come to recognize their own names and respond when called. The relationship is such that the sheep will respond by listening to the shepherd's voice.

Second, there is *his devoted leading of his sheep* (v. 4). The shepherd's task was to seek out good pasture so that the sheep could graze contentedly, secure from the approach of wild beasts that would seek to harm them or precipices that would endanger them. In that part of the world, the custom was for the shepherd to do this not by driving the sheep from behind but by leading them from the front. Jesus is the good shepherd who leads his people safely, even through narrow and dangerous valleys, because he knows the path ahead. Wise sheep (if that is not a contradiction in terms) respond by following joyfully where he leads.

Third, there is *his unique provision for his sheep* (v. 9). Changing the image a little, Jesus next presents himself as the gate of the sheepfold, in which sheep could enjoy protection and from which they could be led to good pasture. In one way, this repeats the previous description about what Jesus does for his sheep, but the accent falls in a different place here. It stresses the response of the sheep to this good shepherd. The privileges of his sheepfold are available to 'all who enter' but not to others. If Jesus can serve his sheep like this, then they should take advantage of it by entering the fold of which he is the only gate. Entering into God's fold means exercising faith in him—in other words, placing total trust in him and him alone. To do so is to take a risk that many people today are not prepared to venture. Many prefer to hedge their bets by putting together a portfolio of religious options and believing in several faith solutions just a little bit, rather than trusting in one. If the risk of choosing God alone is great, though, the rewards are greater, for faith in Jesus as the Christ leads to life, a life that is lived to the full.

Fourth, there is *his voluntary sacrifice for his sheep* (vv. 11–15, 18). The true shepherd is prepared to risk, and even give up, his life for the sake of his sheep. This is the ultimate definition of a good shepherd. Jesus announces that he will do just that—lay down his life for his sheep. The idea seems so strange that he repeats the point, emphasizing that when he eventually surrenders to death, they must remember that he has not done so because he has been forced into it by others (no matter what a superficial reading of his crucifixion might suggest) but because he has voluntarily offered himself in sacrifice. It is in this way that the benefits he bestows on his sheep are won.

Finally, there is *the international nature of his flock* (v. 16). The 'other sheep' to which Jesus refers, who are not 'of this sheep pen', is a reference to the Gentiles. Israel was consistently presented as God's flock, but in future they would no longer be able to claim exclusive rights to be considered as such. Gentiles would be brought into the fold as well. Jesus' comment may have been somewhat enigmatic to those who heard him say it, but as the subsequent story of the Church unfolded, its meaning became clear. He called together a flock of sheep in which the difference between Jew and Gentile no longer mattered. Jesus, the good shepherd, was looking forward to a day when multitudes of people from every nation, tribe and tongue would gather around the throne of God, ironically, to worship himself as the Lamb and celebrate the salvation he had wrought (Revelation 7:9–10).

If there were many leader-shepherds of Israel who had been bad, there was at least one who was good. King David was taken from tending sheep to shepherding the people of Jacob. He 'shepherded them with integrity of heart; with skilful hands he led them' (Psalm

78:72). Under his rule, Israel became stronger, more prosperous and more united than ever before. Many longed for another shepherd to sit on the throne of King David and reign over a kingdom characterized by peace, justice and righteousness. By claiming that he was 'the good shepherd', Jesus, who belonged to the family line of David, was saying that he stood in David's shoes and was David's true heir and successor. At the same time, he was a greater king than David ever was. His glory outshone that of his predecessor by far.

The glory of this shepherd lies in his sheer loving, self-sacrificial goodness. The glory of God is seen radiating from him in the way he seeks for the lost, brings back the strays, binds up the injured and strengthens the weak and does so at the cost of his own life.

Questions

1. What does it mean to you to say 'The Lord is my shepherd' (Psalm 23:1)?

2. How does the image of the shepherd here differ from the popular image we may have today?

17

The glory of the life-giver

JOHN 11:1–44

President Charles de Gaulle once commented, 'Stalin only said one serious thing to me: "In the end, death is the only winner."' It is amazing how much of life is occupied with death: just think how much it dominates our daily news bulletins. Death is the inescapable destination of every one of us. If Jesus was truly to be Lord of all, it was essential that he should conquer death, proving himself to be the life-giver who could stare it in the face and triumph over it. This he did when he himself rose from the grave, but even before then, he showed who was master as he stood at the tomb of his friend Lazarus. In many ways, it was an ordinary situation into which Jesus walked that day in Bethany, but he did so in a most extraordinary manner.

Feel the emotion

In reading this story, our problem is that we know the outcome, so we cannot feel the pathos of those who did not. But John's account spares us none of the raw human emotions that are provoked by death.

There was *grief in the face of human loss*. It is seen in the tearful numbness of Martha and Mary and heard in the half-believing, half-rebuking conversation that they have with Jesus. Both of them blame Jesus for their brother's death. 'If only you had been here…'

they both cry, one after the other (vv. 21, 32). They had enough faith to believe that Jesus could have staved off the approach of death in their brother's body, but not enough to believe that, now death had struck, he could reverse it.

It was a grief that Jesus shared. He was 'deeply moved in spirit and troubled' (v. 33) and wept alongside them (v. 35). His weeping was not the polite identification of a sympathetic actor but the bursting into tears of a grief-stricken man. He felt their loss and was not ashamed, though Lord of all, to express the human emotion of sorrow. His reaction should put an end to the false stifling of grief that sometimes characterizes 'super-spiritual' Christians who feel it wrong to be sorrowful when they lose a loved one because they believe in a resurrection. John Calvin commented, 'Christ's example should be sufficient for rejecting the unbending hardness of the Stoics, for where should we seek for the rule of supreme perfection but in Christ?'[34] And at the tomb of Lazarus, he cried.

There was also *despair in the face of human hopelessness*. The scene seems so desperately bleak because no one present (except Jesus) was expecting a resurrection to take place that day. The only resurrection that the mourners believed in was a general one that would involve them all at the end of the age (v. 24), not the specific one that Lazarus would experience that very day. The presence of Jesus failed to dispel their anguish because, in their eyes, he was only a 'so far Saviour', as Bruce Milne calls him.[35] He could heal the sick but that was the limit of his power: he could not raise the dead. And what is the use of a 'so far Saviour' in the circumstances they faced? All they can do is give vent to loud wailing, no doubt reinforcing their feeling of despair. But it is precisely in situations like this that Jesus shines his compassionate glory. His compassion lay neither in the thoughtfulness of his comforting presence nor in his consoling words, although both of these were evident and would have been helpful. It was the compassion of his transforming action that made the difference.

Hear the claim

Jesus pierced the darkness with his claim to be 'the resurrection and the life' (v. 25). This is his fifth 'I am' saying. In using 'I am', the sacred name for God, with such deliberation, Jesus is making a veiled claim to divinity. The claims he has already made have been absurd enough—unless, of course, they are true. To feed people, enlighten their lives and shepherd them through life, guarding them in his sheepfold, is one thing, but to be 'the resurrection and life' is quite another. Yet throughout the Gospel he has been acting as a life-giver: to a couple in Cana, a ruler of Israel, a woman in Samaria, a lad in Capernaum, a man at Bethesda, and a blind man in the temple. Now he faces a greater challenge in the art of life-giving. Here is the litmus test of whether John's statement was true, that 'in him was life, and that life was the light of all people' (1:4). Could his light and life shine at the tomb of Lazarus?

Jesus is a life-giver not only because he is the creator but also because he is 'the resurrection'. It is he who grants natural life to human beings and then, once death has snuffed it out, grants eternal life. The secret of his power lies in his own resurrection, which reversed, once and for all, the apparent finality of death that no one else until this point (or since) had been able to challenge successfully.

His own resurrection, we should note, would be of a different order than that of Lazarus, whose rising is a pale reflection of what Jesus would undergo. When Lazarus was raised from the tomb, he had to face death again. When Jesus rose from the grave, he was never to face death again. Jesus' resurrection would put death in an entirely new light. Henceforth it would no longer be the ultimate and irreversible enemy. From then on, it would be seen as 'falling asleep' (v. 11), allowing the sleeper to awake later to a new day. Jesus gives the vague Jewish belief in resurrection a new meaning. In raising Lazarus, he brings resurrection near, makes it personal and gives it reality.

The implications of Jesus' claim, which was substantiated by his own resurrection, are of major importance today, when some are imprisoned by grief in the face of death and yet others are attracted to the idea of reincarnation, for which there is no shred of evidence. Jesus' claim is for the present and also for the future. He offers a life that we can begin to taste before the grave but is assured beyond the grave. When the Puritan theologian John Owen was dying, his secretary was composing a letter for him in which he wrote, 'I am still in the land of the living.' Owen instructed him to change it to, 'I am yet in the land of the dying but I shall soon be in the land of the living.' He had a point. The truth is that all who believe in Jesus (this condition is mentioned in verses 26 and 40) are already counted among the living but will one day be even more alive.

See the sign

Most of the 'I am' sayings follow a miracle and help to interpret its significance. In this case, the saying comes first and leads up to the sign. Lazarus has been dead for four days (v. 39). By now his body will be decomposing. According to the Jews, the soul departed from the body after three days in the grave, by which time the complexion had changed and all hope of returning to life had gone. As Jesus stood at the tomb of Lazarus, there was no doubt that his friend was dead. The fact that the miracle took place on the fourth day adds both to the certainty of it and to the astonishment of those who were watching (v. 39). As Bruce Milne comments, 'The greater the challenge, the greater the miracle and the greater the strengthening of his followers' faith as a result; and above all the greater the glory accruing to the Father through it.'[36]

After the stone was removed from the mouth of the tomb, the miracle took place on a single command: 'Lazarus, come out!'(v. 43).

Grasp the motive

No doubt, Jesus was moved by compassion at the loss of his friend and the grief of Lazarus' sisters. But he was motivated by an even deeper drive, that of the glory of God. Twice in the story, the glory of God is mentioned. Jesus tells his disciples that, although they have received a message to say that Lazarus is sick, the illness will not end in his death. The purpose of it, he says, is 'for God's glory so that God's Son may be glorified through it' (v. 4). And verse 40 tells us that when Jesus stood at the tomb, on the brink of raising Lazarus, he said, 'Did I not tell you that if you believed, you would see the glory of God?'

Jesus faces down the last enemy, death, and triumphs over it. In raising Lazarus from the dead, he reveals God's glorious power in the world. Through this miracle, God brings honour to Jesus and causes him to be held in higher esteem by many (v. 45)—but, alas, not all (vv. 47–57). The glory of God the Father and the glory of Jesus his Son is one. Jesus is shown to be not a 'so far Saviour' but one who can save to the uttermost. He is an irrepressible life-giver, whom not even death can defeat.

Questions

1. Paul said that bereaved Christians do not 'grieve like the rest, who have no hope' (1 Thessalonians 4:13). What difference does faith in Jesus Christ make to grief?

2. Imagine yourself at the tomb of Lazarus. How do you think you would have reacted to his resurrection? What would you have thought of Jesus? Would you have seen his glory displayed in the act?

18

The glory of the advancing Messiah

JOHN 12:1–36

Approaching Entebbe airport, where I was due to catch a flight to London after a visit to Christians in northern Uganda, we ran into heavy security. We were made to get out of the vehicle and were thoroughly searched by some soldiers while others conducted a minute inspection of our minibus. Having passed through the various barriers, we discovered that most of the car park in front of the airport was being kept clear. What was going on, we wondered. Why the tight security? Almost two hours later, as I walked across the tarmac to my plane, I found out. There, right beside us, a small private jet landed and out stepped the President of Uganda, closely surrounded by his heavily armed security guards. How different it was when, on what we now call Palm Sunday, Jesus entered into his capital city and was greeted as the Messiah—the king for whom the people of Israel had longed.

The Messiah: anointed by a woman (vv. 1–11)

John's account begins before the triumphal entry with a behind-the-scenes glimpse at what happened over dinner in the home of his friends Mary, Martha and Lazarus. Mary 'took about half a litre of pure nard, an expensive perfume', poured it over Jesus' feet and wiped them with her hair. When Judas protested at the waste involved in this extravagant gesture, Jesus rebuked him, explaining that Mary had intended to save this perfume 'for the day of my burial'. There was a mounting feeling of tension between Jesus and the Jewish authorities, a tension in which Lazarus was caught up (v. 10). In this atmosphere of foreboding, Mary's act anticipated that it would not be long before Jesus' hour came and he would be crucified, dead and buried. She anointed him while he was still alive and could appreciate the love thus demonstrated, instead of leaving the anointing until after his death.

Although John doesn't say as much, there is probably another meaning to this act. It was the job of the high priest to discern the coming of the Messiah and anoint him for office, as one anoints a king on his accession to the throne. The high priest, however, was dismissive of Jesus, ironically saying, not long before, that 'it is better for you that one person die for the people than that the whole nation perish' (11:50). What the high priest failed to see—that Jesus was the Messiah—Mary saw. What the high priest failed to do—anoint the Messiah—Mary did. A woman, considered in those days to be a nobody, helped the Messiah to assume his rightful place.

The Messiah: acclaimed by a crowd (vv. 12–19)

'The next day', Jesus' entry into Jerusalem provoked the most extraordinary scenes and had even more extraordinary meanings attached to it. *Think of the timing.* It took place as the crowd gathered for the feast of the Passover. Tom Wright highlights the significance of that as follows: 'It was Passover time—freedom time! But it was also, as far as they were concerned, kingdom time: the time when the Passover dreams, the great hopes of freedom, of God's sovereignty and saving presence being revealed in quite a unique way, would at last come true.' [37] By entering Jerusalem on that day, Jesus signalled that he was entering into his kingdom, the kingdom of freedom where God would rule, at last, with perfect justice and yet with perfect mercy.

Think of the transport. Jesus rode into the city on a young donkey, an unusual method of transport for a king. I was in Hong Kong not so long ago, when they announced on the news that they were selling the last Governor's car, a beautiful Rolls-Royce, and were looking for offers. That's the more usual method of transport for the kings of the earth; at least, it is these days. In Jesus' day they would have ridden on a white war-horse or in a golden chariot. But Jesus rides on a donkey. He does so to send out a signal that his kingdom will be characterized by humility and gentleness instead of power and might. He also does so to fulfil the Old Testament scriptures (Genesis 49:11; Zechariah 9:9), which prophesied that when the true ruler of Judah came, he would arrive riding on a donkey.

Think of the greeting. The crowd celebrated Jesus' arrival by waving palm branches in their hands, just as, 200 years previously, their ancestors had greeted the Jewish hero Judas Maccabeus after he had defeated the Syrians and made his way into Jerusalem to cleanse the temple. From one perspective, the words they shouted were the typical words with which all pilgrims were welcomed as they arrived for the feast. 'Hosanna', which means 'God help us' and 'save us now', occurs in the Greek translation of Psalm 118:25–26 and was used regularly as a greeting. But into that innocuous greeting the people weave words that are political dynamite, for they proclaim Jesus as coming 'in the name of the Lord' and as 'the King of Israel'. They are, in other words, identifying him as the one whom they have longed to see, who will sit on the throne of David and rule over his reconstituted kingdom. That meant Jesus was a real threat to the power of Rome and of those Jews who had allied themselves with Rome's imperialism.

It was only when the disciples looked back at these events, John admits, that they understood what was really going on (v. 16). In confessing their slowness to grasp the significance of the occasion, John creates a link with what follows by saying that they only understood 'after Jesus was glorified'—a reference to his crucifixion.

The theme of the glorification of Jesus is to assume increasing importance from now on.

The Messiah: approached by some Greeks (vv. 20–22)

Feeling impotent in the face of the popular support that Jesus received, the Pharisees complained that 'the whole world has gone after him'. Then, to illustrate the point, the next thing we read is about 'some Greeks' who want to have an interview with Jesus. They must have been 'God-fearers', the technical name for Gentiles who were attracted to Judaism and followed it as much as they could, for they were in Jerusalem to join in the celebration of the Passover feast.

Their request triggered a deep response in Jesus. To this point, his ministry had been confined to the Jewish people. Their request meant that, as the Pharisees had ironically suggested, it was about to go into a new orbit and become international. If Jesus had acquiesced to the request of the Greeks, and to the others that would have followed, his celebrity status would have taken his ministry in a very different direction from the one God had planned. It would have diverted him from going to his cross and dying for sin and would have left us with a sensation to follow but not a saviour to trust. Their request made Jesus realize that 'the hour has come for the Son of Man to be glorified'. Astonishingly, God's way of revealing the ultimate honour of his Son was to reveal it on a cross.

Jesus uses three illustrations to explain the paradox of how someone can be glorified by being crucified. The point of crucifying criminals was to shame them, not to honour them. So what can Jesus mean? He speaks of a seed needing to die in order to bear fruit, of people losing their lives in order to find them, and of a servant following him (even to death) in order to be honoured by his Father. 'The paradox,' Michael Ramsey remarked, 'that Passion and glory are one will be learnt only in the practical obedience of discipleship.'[38]

The Messiah: affirmed by heaven (vv. 23–36)

The awesome significance of the moment strikes Jesus so hard that he naturally shrinks from what he knows lies ahead. Here is John's version of his suffering in Gethsemane. Such is the struggle Jesus faces that a voice of affirmation is heard, breaking in from heaven to encourage him. Jesus longs to honour God's name, no matter what the personal cost. The voice assures him that it will be so: 'I have glorified it, and will glorify it again.' Here, too, is John's version of the mount of transfiguration. Gethsemane and transfiguration join hands. Passion and glory are united. The one is impossible without the other.

With the coming of the Greeks, the final act of the revelation of Jesus' glory has begun. Active public ministry ceases, a private time of ministry to his closest disciples commences, and the glory of the cross casts its shadow over all.

Questions

1. Riding into Jerusalem as Jesus did was a political act. Is it possible to separate religion and politics?

2. How far does the teaching of this chapter subvert our normal understanding of 'glory' or 'honour'? What challenges does it present to us to live free from conventional understandings of status and honour today?

19

The glory of the humble servant

JOHN 13:1–17

With John 13 we move into a new phase of Jesus' ministry. The crowds recede into the background; the public teaching and miraculous signs are past. Instead, we find ourselves in an intimate setting in which Jesus imparts his final instruction ·to his inner circle. The previous twelve chapters occupy two and a half years of ministry. These chapters occupy only a day or so.

Chapters 13—17 are sometimes called 'the book of glory' because the vocabulary of glory becomes more common and the concern with glory more central. Yet the glory of Jesus is made known in the most surprising of ways. Jews associated glory with God's powerfully radiant and unapproachably awesome presence, as when the law was given on Sinai or the temple was dedicated under Solomon. Here we learn that Jesus' glory is most truly manifest not through his strength and power but in his humility, suffering, weakness and shame. This 'book of glory' could have no more fitting introduction than the account of when Jesus adopts the role of a humble servant and washes the feet of his disciples.

The glory of his knowledge (vv. 1–3)

What Jesus does is even more amazing because of what he knows: 'Jesus knew that the time had come for him to leave this world and go to the Father.' Throughout his ministry, he had shown an amazing and accurate knowledge about people and situations, from the day when he first met Nathanael (1:48) to the day he stood at the tomb of Lazarus (11:42). But here his knowledge is deeper still. He knows that his departure is near (v. 1), his betrayer is close (v. 2), his power is secure (v. 3) and his disciples are chosen (v. 18). His knowledge contrasts strongly with the ignorance of his disciples, mentioned several times in this chapter (vv. 7, 12, 17).

Jesus knew that he would shortly face the agony of betrayal by a friend, a false trial and an unjust execution. He was a victim. He might, therefore, have been understandably preoccupied with his own concerns and feelings. Yet, knowing what he does, he deliberately (as the little word 'so' at the start of verse 4 tells us) gets up from the table and plays the role of a servant.

The glory of his love (v. 1)

The reason Jesus acts as he does is because he is motivated by love. Having loved his disciples to this point, he loves them, as the original words might mean, either 'to the very end' (not stopping short in time) or 'to the full extent' (not stopping short in quality). Here is an unconditional and unfailing love, which contrasts strongly with the love that many exhibited in Jesus' time. Their culture taught the importance of reciprocal love. You gave when you were sure that you would get something back as a result. You gave when it was worth your while. But there was no obvious return in this for Jesus. His disciples, far from even standing by him in the next day or so, would desert him. But he still loved them. Here is grace at work, a love that goes beyond all reason. How different is the conditional, calculating or convenient love in which we often indulge.

The glory of his humility (vv. 2–17)

The heart of the story, however, concerns not Jesus' inward state of mind but his outward actions. At some point in the meal, he left the table, stripped off his outer garments, took a basin and a towel and washed his disciples' feet. It was the task for the lowest slave to perform. Indeed, it was so menial that Jewish slaves were exempted from performing the duty. While it was a thoughtful gesture for a host to arrange for his guests' feet to be washed after they had made their dusty journey to his table, it was not always done, and the host would certainly not perform the duty himself. Hence Don Carson's comment that Jesus' 'act of humility is as unnecessary as it is stunning'.[39]

The action is to be understood on three different levels, as a dramatic prophecy, an acted parable and a spiritual lesson.

It is *a dramatic prophecy, enacting the future*. The phrases in this passage are carefully chosen to echo others in the Gospel that relate to the cross. Jesus' removal of his outer garment is a foretaste of the way his clothes will be taken from him at Golgotha (19:23). The same vocabulary was used about the good shepherd laying down his life (10:11, 15, 17). Similarly, when we read that he 'put on his clothes and returned to his place', we are reminded of Jesus' earlier comment that he would lay down his life 'only to take it up again' (10:17, 18).

The clearest echoes, however, are heard not in John's writings but in Paul's. In Philippians 2:5–11, Paul tells us, step by step, the meaning of what Jesus acted out in that upper room. Jesus got up from his rightful place at the table, just as he 'did not consider equality with God something to be grasped'. He 'took off his outer clothing', just as he 'made himself nothing'. He 'wrapped a towel round his waist… and began to wash his disciples' feet', just as he took on 'the very nature of a servant'. He 'poured water into a basin', just as he was to pour out his life, becoming 'obedient to death— even death on a cross!' Finally, 'when he had finished… he returned to his place', just as after his death 'God exalted him to the highest place'. This leads John Stott to say, 'For me there is no clearer or more compelling evidence of the deity of Jesus than the extraordinary paradox between his lofty claims and his lowly conduct.'[40]

Before it happens, then, Jesus predicts his cross in dramatic form.

It is *an acted parable of the cleansing he provides*. If the drama is a foreshadowing of his cross, it is also a parable of salvation. From earliest days, sin was understood to be like dirt, polluting and defiling people's lives. To deal with it, people needed to be cleansed, and to be cleansed they needed a cleansing agent. Just as we use soap to remove dirt from our hands, so another detergent is needed to remove the dirt from our hearts. Throughout the Bible it is clear that God's chosen cleansing agent was blood, but all its earlier uses point to, and are mere anticipations of, the blood that Jesus shed on his cross.

Here Jesus washes his disciples' feet, symbolically cleansing them from the dirt that defiles. Peter, typically, protests. Perhaps he is embarrassed that his master should perform such a humble task. Perhaps he wants to be self-sufficient. He can wash his own feet, thank you very much. After all he has seen Jesus do and heard him teach, he still thinks he knows better than his master. But Jesus rebukes him and hints at the spiritual cleansing needed for anyone to be one of his followers. Peter then, again typically, overreacts. 'In that case,' he says, 'don't stop with the feet. I'll have a fuller wash, please.' Jesus' reply is to the effect that you don't always need to have a full bath. Having bathed, there is just the need, as we would say, to keep your hands clean. In making this distinction, Jesus is speaking of the way in which we receive, at conversion and through regeneration, a fundamental, once-for-all cleansing from sin. The defilement of our lives has been dealt with, but there is still the need to seek daily cleansing for the sins we subsequently commit.

It is *a spiritual lesson about the example he leaves*. If, so far, we have been digging beneath the surface a little to understand the meaning of Jesus' action, there is another meaning that lies on the surface and is perfectly clear. Jesus says, 'I have set you an example that you should do as I have done for you.' From this time, the key symbols for Christian service, and especially for Christian leaders, would be a towel and a basin. They are symbolic because Jesus does not mean us to fulfil his command literally (it would make no sense in modern Western societies) but he does mean us to apply his command

111

dynamically. The implication is that we are to take the position of lowliness in our relations with one another, being eager to do the menial tasks and serve the interests of others rather than being conscious of our rights, our status and the way others should serve us. But Donald Kraybill, anxious about the way we too easily turn these commands into pious thoughts instead of real actions, reminds us that the towel and the basin 'are not only symbols. They are the means by which something is actually done. These tools define our trade.' [41]

It's a hard lesson to learn, even though modelled and taught by the most perfect teacher who ever existed. Our concern with 'self' makes us constantly want to soften Jesus' instruction, but in Jesus' action we see true glory. As T.W. Manson said, 'In the kingdom of God service is not a stepping-stone to nobility: it *is* nobility, the only kind of nobility that is recognized.' [42] It is not a stepping-stone to glory; it's the only kind of glory there is. Truly, there is glory in being a humble servant.

Questions

1. Like the disciples, we are often caught out by Jesus in our ignorance. He doesn't behave as we might expect him to do. How has the portrait of Jesus in John's Gospel surprised you?

2. What acts of humble service have you engaged in recently that might display the glory of Christ in a needy world? If the answer is none, think about what you could start doing to serve others.

20

The glory of the pathfinder

JOHN 14:1–14

I stand in awe of the great adventurers and explorers who forge untrodden paths to new worlds. What was it, for example, in 1858, that drove John Speke, a British Army officer, to trek uncomfortably for months through the uncharted territories of East Africa in search of the source of the River Nile, until he came upon (and named) Lake Victoria? What was it that caused the space pioneers to risk their lives to enter an alien atmosphere or inspired Neil Armstrong to be the first to set foot on the moon in 1969? The world benefits from their discoveries and applauds their courage.

Part of the glory of Jesus lies in his work as a pioneer—the pathfinder who forges a new way to an eternal home for us. Here, in one of his best-known sayings, he claims, 'I am the way and the truth and the life. No one comes to the Father except through me.'

An essential way

For the disciples, finding the way was essential. They had a vague idea of God and of the path they had to follow to meet him. They believed in God, as much as any Jew—well, Jewish man—would. But the reality was that they were really lost in the fog. For all the religious instruction they had received, they were like the Israel whose tragic situation Isaiah described when he wrote, 'Like the blind we grope along the wall, feeling our way like people without eyes. At midday we stumble as if it were twilight; among the strong, we are like the dead' (Isaiah 59:10). The disciples needed someone to provide them with a way to God that would disperse the fog and show them clearly where to go.

Jesus invited them to have more than a nebulous trust in God. He invited them to trust in him as the one who would prepare the way for them so that eventually they could join with him on his final journey to his Father. And when they asked what God was like, Jesus told them again that if they wanted to know God they should look at him. He alone could give them the direction they sought. If others made such a claim, we would dismiss them as sad or mad or deluded by their own arrogance, but when Jesus makes the claim it is not easily dismissed. It rings true.

An actual way

Jesus is the pioneer who goes through the gate of death and is the first to experience resurrection and ascension into heaven. The path he forges is the path his followers will themselves follow one day.

His claim is even more particular than that, however. In saying, 'I am the way', he was more accurately saying, 'I myself am the road', as J.B. Philips put it so helpfully in his translation of the New Testament.[43] Jesus was claiming to be neither a teacher of the way nor a mere signpost, nor even a guide pointing to the correct road. He was claiming to be the vehicle that would conduct people to their destination or the very highway on which people must walk to reach the home of God. He is not the messenger but the message. He is more than the pathfinder: he is the path.

An effective way

The simple words of verse 6 are capable of being translated in a different way from that with which most of us are familiar. Jesus may not have meant that he was three different things—firstly the way, secondly the truth and thirdly the life—but that he was one thing: 'a true and living way'. Some 'ways' are full of obstacles and hidden pitfalls. Others seem to promise much but quickly lead nowhere, petering out in a dead end. Many promises made by contemporary advertisers offer us the possibility of transformed and troublefree lives but are nothing short of deceitful. In a world of fraudulent offers and empty promises, it is vital to know that the way we follow is genuine and life-enhancing rather than spurious and life-reducing.

When we put it like this, some of the great themes of the Gospel are pressed into service as we learn what sort of way Jesus is. He is the genuine, reliable, trustworthy way just as we would expect from one who was 'full of grace and truth' (1:14). As the living way, he leads not to dead orthodoxy, burdensome religion or oppressive legalism, but to full and rich living in relation to God.

I recall visiting a remote cottage in Wales one dark November evening, trying, without too much success, to find my way through the wind and rain while driving. I was not sure I was reading the map correctly and was even less confident about identifying the names of Welsh villages accurately. But then the owner of the remote cottage caught me up in his car and led the way. He had been there many times before and knew the way backwards! What relief I felt as I gladly followed him. Here was a guide who was trustworthy and, in the weariness of a late evening, able to revive my flagging spirits.

An exclusive way

There is usually more than one way to reach a destination, but Jesus adds to the claim he has made (which was already faith-stretching enough) another hard-to-believe factor. He claims to be not *a* way to God but *the* way: 'No one comes to the Father except through me.' He is the exclusive introduction agency. If we want a famous person to attend a function that we are arranging, we will often use an intermediary who knows the person to pass on our request and encourage them to accept the invitation. Jesus is the sole inter-mediary between ourselves and God. He alone can broker the introduction and restore the relationship.

Few, of course, will accept such exclusive claims today. Financially, we put together a portfolio of options so that we spread our assets to avoid undue risk. Spiritually, many do the same. A little bit of trust in Jesus is mixed with a pinch of Eastern meditation, a dash of old paganism and a few grammes of belief in reincarnation, cooked in the oven of broad-mindedness towards all religions, no matter how contradictory. While we should live peacefully alongside neighbours of other faiths, this overall 'pick and mix' approach reminds me of Dorothy L. Sayers' comment on tolerance, which she described as 'the sin that believes in nothing, cares for nothing, seeks to know nothing, interferes with nothing, enjoys nothing, hates nothing, finds purpose in nothing, lives for nothing and remains alive because there is nothing for which to die'.[44]

But Jesus will have none of it. There are not several roads that lead to this destination—only one, and he is that road. It makes perfect sense in the light of all that has been said in John's Gospel up to now, for Jesus alone has come from God and he alone knows what he is talking about.

An authentic way

Philip, understandably, wades in to ask for further clarification and for some evidence to justify Jesus' claim. Jesus seems rather dis-appointed that his friends should require such confirmation. Have his life and teaching not been evidence enough of his authenticity? Is there not such an obvious and intimate connection between him and his Father that the disciples can see that the words he speaks and the deeds he does can only come from God? If they remain unconvinced, Jesus argues, then they should look at the bottom line: 'at least believe on the evidence of the miracles themselves'

(v. 11). Surely the miracles would convince the sceptical disciples that he, and he alone, is the authentic way to God.

Thomas à Kempis famously expressed the words of Jesus like this:

Follow thou me: 'I am the way the truth and the life.' Without the way, there is no going; without the truth, there is no knowing; without the life, there is no living. I am the way, which thou must follow; the truth, which thou oughtest trust; the life which thou oughtest hope for. I am the inviolable way; the truth infallible; the life that cannot end. I am the straightest way; the highest truth; the true life, the life blessed, the life uncreated. If thou remain in my way, thou shalt know the truth, and the truth shall make thee free, and thou shalt lay hold of eternal life.[45]

One of the delights of living in recent times has been the opportunity to visit parts of the world that were inaccessible to our grandparents or great-grandparents. We can enjoy the wonder of these sights because pathfinders went before and opened up the way. They often did so at great cost to themselves and their teams, and many paid the ultimate price. To Jesus belongs the honour of being the ultimate pathfinder, opening up the way to his Father in heaven and forging a way through sin to lead us to an eternal home. But he, too, did so at the expense of his own life. When he said to his disciples that he was 'going there to prepare a place for you', he was alluding to his crucifixion, resurrection and ascension. When he said, 'I will come back and take you to be with me', he was speaking of his second coming. We must be ready to make this final journey when he calls.

Questions

1. What do you think of the exclusive claims of Jesus? Is he really the only way? If so, what impact should this have on the way we live and witness?

2. Where are you on the journey with Jesus the pathfinder? Are you ready to die and enter the house he has prepared for you at any time?

21

The glory of the fruitful vine

JOHN 15:1–17

I really cannot stand gardening, because I never seem to have the time to do it. When I do get out the tools and have a go, my first task is to fight back the wilderness. I'm sure I would like it better if I ever got beyond this stage to a more positive task. After all, I enjoy it when the flowers and the fruit grow. One of my predecessors planted a peach tree. To see the peaches form, develop and ripen and then to taste what has grown in your own garden is marvellous. Even so, agricultural imagery doesn't come naturally to me; but it did to Jesus and he makes use of it when he speaks of himself as 'the true vine'. There's more to it than just a handy illustration, for here, as David Gooding puts it, is 'a metaphor with a history'.[46]

The picture Jesus uses

The vine had long been used as *a symbol of Israel*. The lush vines of the Kidron valley could produce clusters of grapes as much as two metres long. The temple had an image of a golden vine trailing over its porch, and during the revolt against the Romans the Jews marked their coinage with a vine. They were not only picking up an obvious symbol from their own times but also drawing on the many allusions in their scriptures to Israel as a vine.

On the one hand, the ancient writers had chosen the vine to point out how rich God's provision had been for Israel. Psalm

80:8–9 spoke of God bringing 'a vine out of Egypt', which was planted and took root in ground that had been carefully cleared. Isaiah 5:1–2 spoke of Israel as the choicest of vines, planted on a fertile hillside from which all rubble had been removed. Ezekiel 17:8 used the same picture, adding that alongside the good soil there was an abundant supply of water.

On the other hand, these very same writers used the image to speak of the failure of Israel to yield the fruit that God expected and which it had every opportunity to produce. Let Isaiah speak for them all: 'Then [God] looked for a crop of good grapes, but it yielded only bad fruit' (Isaiah 5:2). Israel had become self-indulgent in enjoying its favourable place in God's world and had failed in the mission that God had planned for it. Hosea 10:1 condemned the nation as 'a spreading vine [that] brought forth fruit for himself'. Where Israel had failed in her calling, Jesus was now succeeding.

The image had already been alluded to when Jesus performed *a sign at Cana*. As Imentioned before, most of the signs in John's Gospel have an explanation or discussion attached to them. Perhaps this is the long-delayed discussion of the miracle of changing water into wine, when his disciples saw him reveal his glory. Is Jesus explaining that the old ritual laws of Israel, symbolized by the pots of water, are now being replaced by the new wine of his kingdom of abundant grace? Surely it is the failure of Israel and of those laws that he has in mind when he speaks of branches being cut off and thrown away when they do not bear the expected fruit.

The point Jesus makes

The vine, as Bruce Milne points out, is not really a pretty object. You wouldn't use it for decoration.[47] It is a utilitarian plant that has only one use: to produce grapes. That is the particular role of the branches, fed with life from the roots and trunk of the vine. Jesus tells us that bearing fruit is our business, but what is the fruit we are meant to bear? Again, this metaphor is well used elsewhere in the Bible.

There is the fruit-bearing involved in *witnessing to God's salvation*. Isaiah 27:6, for example, uses the image of a vine to envisage a day when 'Jacob will take root, Israel will bud and blossom and fill all the world with fruit'. On this occasion, the fruit is the announcement of God's salvation, his plan for dealing with sin, from which all nations were to benefit.

Then there is the fruit-bearing involved in *working for social justice*. The short passage in Isaiah 5 that introduces the image of Israel as a vine concludes in verse 7: God 'looked for justice, but saw bloodshed; for righteousness, but heard cries of distress'. The Israelites had failed to live by and stand for that which was right. Instead of peace, they resorted to violence. Instead of justice, they resorted to corruption. Instead of protecting the vulnerable, they resorted to abusing them for their own ends. The fruit of mission is not only evangelism but also social justice.

There is also the fruit-bearing involved in *growing in personal character*. In Galatians 5:22–23, Paul speaks of the virtues of 'love, joy, peace, patience, kindness, goodness, faithfulness, gentleness and self-control' as 'the fruit of the Spirit'. These few words contain a wealth of truth. They describe the sort of persons God longs for us to be. By using the single word 'fruit' instead of the plural 'fruits', Paul is reminding us that we cannot pick and choose between these qualities. We cannot be specialists in joy while never exercising self-control. We might envisage the image as that of a blended fruit drink in which the taste of one ingredient flavours the others. Paul teaches us that although effort is required on our part, it is the Holy Spirit who provides the life deep within us, which produces the fruit.

The principles Jesus teaches

It is evident that Jesus' primary concern is not with the quantity of fruit produced but with its quality. Verse 16, for example, speaks about his desire that the fruit 'will last' rather than become rotten as soon as it is harvested or even while it is still on the vine. How is that quality to be produced? He gives us four secrets in spiritual horticulture.

First, it will involve *pruning*. Verse 2 refers to the habit of double pruning, which was practised in Jesus' day. During April and May, dead branches incapable of bearing fruit would have been cut out and thrown away. Then, in July and August, weaker branches would be pinched out to allow the stronger ones to produce full and healthy clusters of grapes. If we are to be top-quality fruit bearers for Jesus, we should expect to experience God's gracious pruning of our lives. The kind of knife he uses will vary. It may be a verse from scripture that convicts us, a friend who criticizes us or circumstances that constrain us. Conflict, hardship, failure and even doubts are used by God to discipline us and produce fruit.

Second, it will involve *remaining*, as verses 4–5 teach. It is obvious that no branch is capable of producing fruit once it is cut off from the vine. It lacks the source of life that alone can generate the fruit. No computer can function when it is cut off from the power supply, the electricity needed to make it work. So it is with us in spiritual terms. The simple secret is to stay close and stay connected to Jesus. To do that, we must spend time with him and cultivate companionship with him. We must be careful not to mistake this for cosy sentimentality, though, for, as verses 7 and 10 state, the only way to stay close to Jesus is to engage in deliberate and active obedience to his teaching.

Third, it will involve *praying*. Verse 7 appears to give us a blank cheque as far as prayer is concerned: 'ask whatever you wish, and it will be given you'. But we should not miss the context. These words are spoken to those who abide in Jesus, and those who do this will not be making foolish, self-centred requests or asking for anything that will dishonour God. Nonetheless, it does encourage us as his disciples to have confidence to ask for what we know will glorify him.

Fourth, it will involve *loving*. When, from verse 9 onwards, Jesus begins to talk to his disciples about loving each other, he is not introducing a new subject but continuing to unfold the nature of successful fruit-bearing. This is really no great mystery; it does not lie in strategies, techniques, programmes and methods. The secret is simply to love. Any church can do that. It doesn't have to be rich or large or hi-tech; it just has to love. That means shunning conflict, politics, bitterness, resentment, judgmentalism and coldness. It means accepting one another in grace and then seeing the transforming power of love at work.

The purpose Jesus has

Why does Jesus say all this? He says it because he is concerned to bring honour to his Father. Bearing fruit, he says, 'is to my Father's glory'. It is not so that our name should be known, our projects successful and our own kingdoms built, but so that God's name should be made known and lifted high. John Stott reminds us, 'The highest of all missionary motives is neither obedience to the Great Commission, nor love for sinners who are alienated and perishing but rather zeal—burning and passionate zeal—for the glory of Jesus Christ' and of the Father, too.[48]

Questions

1. Reflecting on your own life, what type of lasting fruit have you borne? Ask yourself honestly whether your motive has been the glory of God or merely to further your own reputation.

2. In the church's experience, persecution might be considered as one form of pruning. Opposition often leads to a vibrant church. Is the rather weak church of the West in need of pruning? If so, what form of pruning might serve the glory of God?

22

The glory of the absent Saviour

JOHN 16:1–33

Christians often say that it must have been so much easier to be a disciple of Jesus while he was alive on earth, so it comes as something of a shock to hear him telling his disciples that it is to their advantage that he is leaving them (v. 7). It was not that his withdrawal was to save them further pain or embarrassment, but so that the next phase of God's salvation story might commence. Here we see the glory of the Saviour who, for a time, is hidden from view.

The glory of the giving Saviour (vv. 5–15)

It is a sobering experience to have to clear out the possessions of someone who has just died. The clothes that looked good on them now seem pretty worn and sad; the possessions they treasured may not be worth much to others; the photos they took, and the papers and diaries they wrote, usually have little significance now that they are no longer around. If they live on, as it were, they do so through their children.

For Jesus, it is totally different. The fact that he is no longer around does not mean that his life has been brought to an end. Rather, it opens up a new, more significant phase of his activity on earth, one which is not confined in space and time, and which he now conducts through 'the Counsellor' whom he sends in his place. 'Counsellor' is a difficult word to express in English. Some resort to transliterating the Greek letters and call him 'the Paraclete'. The word means a lawyer, one who is called in to stand alongside a defendant and give them active help and support in their cause. This Paraclete, however, is not so much called in as sent in.

In introducing the Counsellor, Jesus sets out the new relationships that will be forged after his withdrawal from the world.

There is the relationship between *Jesus and the Counsellor*. They have the closest of relationships. Point by point, what is said of Jesus during his time on earth is said of the Counsellor afterwards. He is the alter ego of Jesus, and they are never in conflict or competition. Jesus explains that the Counsellor 'will bring glory to me by taking from what is mine and making it known to you'. As Tom Smail writes, 'When the Holy Spirit moves, the destination is more important than the emotion, what we feel matters less than where we are going... The Spirit moves us towards Christ.'[49] Any spiritual teaching that distracts us from Jesus and anything that makes us less like Jesus cannot come from his Spirit.

There is the relationship between *the world and the Counsellor*. The Counsellor acts not only as the defence counsel for Jesus' followers but also as the prosecution counsel against the world. Verses 8–11 begin with the words, 'he will convict the world of guilt...' This means that he will expose the lie about Jesus—the lie that Jesus is a charlatan, which the world has believed and circulated—with a view to bringing about the world's repentance. If the Counsellor did not play this role, the world would continue in its blissful but fatal ignorance.

Three particular accusations are listed on the charge sheet. First, there is 'sin', the heart of which lies in unbelief. Then there is 'righteousness', a word that comes from a law court where the judge decides who is right. The world has decided that Jesus is in the wrong, but this cannot be so, for his 'going to the Father' proves that God was on his side and so he, not the world, is vindicated. Finally, there is 'judgment'. The world has passed a judgment on Jesus and condemned him, but the events that are soon to follow will prove its judgment false. The one who is truly condemned is

Jesus' chief opponent, the one who inspires opposition to him—'the prince of this world'.

There is the relationship between *the disciples and the Counsellor*. In verses 12–15, attention turns to the role that the Holy Spirit plays in relation to the disciples, where he is the Spirit of truth (see 14:17; 15:26; 16:13). The disciples may wonder how they will manage without Jesus, but the Spirit will be a sufficient resource, drawing them back to his teaching and spelling it out more and more fully for them as the need arises.

The glory of the resurrected Saviour (vv. 16–32)

Jesus often seems to speak in riddles. The riddle here is in verse 16: 'In a little while you will see me no more, and then after a little while you will see me.' He sounds as if he is playing a game of hide-and-seek. It becomes clear, however, that he is alluding to his resurrection. That has been the missing piece in the disciples' understanding. They were all too well aware of the opposition Jesus faced and it didn't take much to realize that the authorities were determined to do away with him. But a Messiah who ended up being crucified was no Messiah at all in their book. It just didn't make sense. Once the resurrection is introduced into the discussion, though, everything changes. Jesus uses a number of approaches to explain this fuller picture to them.

To begin with, he speaks of pregnancy, in which *new life is created through bearing pain*. When Jesus is crucified, the world will rejoice, thinking it has got rid of a troublemaker, but the disciples will grieve. Yet both reactions will be premature, for the story is not yet over. Without enduring the pain of childbirth, no woman can have the joy of holding her newborn baby in her arms. Similarly, without the pain of the cross, Jesus would not have been able to have the joy of defeating death and rising from it to pioneer a new way—the way of resurrection life.

Then Jesus explains that the disciples will soon experience a *new intimacy created through his rising again*. Until now, their relationship with God the Father has been somewhat hesitant and indirect. They haven't asked him for anything, haven't understood him clearly and haven't known him with any sense of assurance. After the resurrection, though, things will change. The disciples will find a new confidence in prayer and a new clarity in their understanding of God. Above all, they will discover a new assurance of his love for them: 'the Father himself loves you because you have loved me and have believed that I came from God'. Their faithfulness and trust in him will lead them to become confident members of God's family, at home in his company and sure of his love.

Jesus signals that he is about to complete his mission on earth. He is 'leaving the world and going back to the Father' (v. 28). He does so not to escape from further conflict, because the road he takes lies through the valley of suffering and execution, but because his task on earth is done. Within a matter of days, all that he came to do will be completed. Phase one of God's rescue mission, as it were—the phase that involves the Son's mission on earth—will be over, and phase two—the phase that involves the Spirit's mission on earth—will commence. The public proclamation that his task is gloriously completed will shortly be announced from the cross as Jesus cries, 'It is finished' (19:30).

The glory of the conquering Saviour (v. 33)

Jesus does not want to leave his disciples under any misapprehension. The fact that he has completed his work does not mean that they will be free from trouble in the future. Nor does it mean that the world will instantly see how wrong it was about Jesus and come to believe in him. The misunderstanding, conflict and rejection he experienced will be replayed in the disciples' lives, as well as in those of their successors around the world, again and again. If what Jesus has been saying is true, about new life coming to birth through pain, then we shouldn't really be surprised. It can't happen any other way.

In spite of all appearances to the contrary, however, there is one truth to which the disciples must cling. 'Take heart!' Jesus concludes. 'I have overcome the world.' The truth—the ultimate truth that will one day be revealed for everyone to see—is that the final victor, who has defeated all opposition and reigns supreme over all, is the one who was nailed to a cross and apparently defeated. Jesus' crucifixion wasn't a mistake due to circumstances beyond his control or an unfortunate accident. It was God's way of reclaiming his world from the captivity of his enemies and reestablishing his legitimate, gracious and liberating reign once more. Jesus' crucifixion lay on the path to his resurrection and exaltation to the right hand of God.

The fateful hours that were to follow this conversation would be dark indeed, but Jesus was not defeated in those hours. He looked beyond them to the time when he himself would be absent from the earth. Only then would his disciples understand his true glory. Jesus overcame the darkness in the world by his light, the sin in the world by his grace, the shame in the world by his honour, the death in the world by his resurrection and the usurping ruler of the world by triumphing over him on the cross.

Questions

1. Do you sometimes think that it would have been easier to follow Jesus when he was physically present on earth? If so, how convincing do you find his argument that we have the greater good of the Holy Spirit with us?

2. Can you trace the work of the Holy Spirit in the world (outside the walls of the church), fulfilling his mission and bringing glory to Christ? If not, what do you make of the way the gospel flourished in many of the lands previously dominated by communism, where Christianity was banned?

23

The glory of the submissive intercessor

JOHN 17:1–26

In John 17, we stand on sacred ground as we overhear Jesus talking intimately with his Father, his ministry on earth drawing to a climax. It is often said that Jesus is praying here in his role as high priest. That is not a bad description, provided we understand that the high priest's task was not only to intercede for others but also to offer sacrifices on behalf of others. Here, Jesus prays for his disciples, but his initial concern is to dedicate his own life to the Father as a sacrifice that is about to be offered on the cross. This is John's recollection of what went on in the garden of Gethsemane.

The prayer falls naturally into three sections: Jesus prays for himself and for his Father's glory (vv. 1–5), he prays for his disciples and their protection (vv. 6–19), and he prays for his Church and its unity (vv. 20–26). Many of the great themes of John's Gospel are mentioned in this prayer, but the thread on which every jewel hangs is the theme of glory. Mentioned six times in the chapter, 'glory' is found here in a more concentrated form than in any other part of the Gospel. Let's consider how it weaves its way through the chapter.

Glory sought: the glory of his death (v. 1)

The German theologian Rudolph Bultmann pointed out that the whole of the prayer is contained in this first petition: 'Glorify your

Son, that your Son may glorify you.' It expresses Jesus' desire to honour God in his death as much as he has done in his life. We know that Jesus is referring particularly to his death here because he begins with the words, 'the hour has come'. When he has spoken of 'his time' or 'his hour' previously, it has always referred to the cross. Now that this time has arrived, he prays for steadfast courage not to flinch in the face of certain torture and horrible death.

It is an extraordinary request. Humanly speaking, there was little glory to be found in crucifixion. As a method of execution, it had been designed to shame and humiliate its victims, not to honour and dignify them. Yet Jesus presents himself as a sacrifice on the altar of humiliation and prays that his offering may be acceptable to God and may bring honour to his Father by accomplishing the work of salvation.

Glory displayed: the glory of his ministry (v. 4)

In seeking strength to honour God right to the end, Jesus points out that he is only seeking to continue what he has been doing all along. He is not suddenly starting to glorify God. Throughout his life, he has been doing just that through his teaching, in his miracles and his relationships—indeed, through every part of his being. John verified as much with his eyewitness testimony (1:14). Although Jesus lived as a human being, the whole purpose of his incarnation had been to bring acclaim to his Father and cause people to revere him. This purpose had been wonderfully fulfilled. Glory had been brought to God's name. God's splendour had been displayed in the world, his magnificence revealed, and many had come to believe in and worship him as a result of what they had seen.

Glory possessed: the glory of his deity (v. 5)

Now that the task on earth is about to be completed, Jesus prays for a restoration of the glory that he himself enjoyed in the Father's presence before his incarnation as a human being. This can only mean that Jesus existed before he was born as a human baby in Bethlehem. Verse 24 underlines this point: his glory is a glory that he had 'before the creation of the world'. This raises Jesus to a different plane than that of any other man. It cannot mean that God saw Jesus as a human being, who so pleased him by the way he lived that he was later adopted in a special way by God and was raised to share God's throne with him. It must mean that Jesus was uniquely related to God from eternity, as his one and only Son, and was therefore uniquely qualified to be the Saviour of a fallen world.

Glory ascribed: the glory of his disciples (v. 10)

Once he has dedicated himself in prayer to God, Jesus prays for his disciples. His death, resurrection and ascension will have major implications for them. The hostility he has experienced will then be directed towards them as his disciples. 'The world' (by which John means 'the world system' and those who control it and live by it, standing in opposition to God) will ensure that their lives are subject to opposition, discomfort and persecution. Hostility was inevitable because the disciples of Jesus would never belong to 'the world'—and 'the world' cannot bear non-conformists. While he was with them, Jesus was able to afford them protection, but once he is absent, this will no longer be so. Consequently, he prays that the Father himself will protect them.

While Jesus is asking for this protection from his Father, he makes a most surprising statement. He says that 'glory has come to me through them' (v. 10). What we know of the disciples causes us to do a double-take here! What can Jesus mean? The disciples have been slow to understand, often lacking in faith and, on occasions, downright obtuse. If Jesus had wanted to enhance his glory on earth, we cannot help but feel that he could have chosen a better group to support him and fan his reputation into flame. Yet, for all their faults, these disciples believed when others didn't, and they stayed with him when others deserted him. He had derived pleasure from their friendship and resilience from their discipleship. As Don Carson comments, 'The extent to which Jesus has been glorified in the lives of his disciples is still pathetically slim compared with what will yet be, but it is infinitely better than what he has received from the world.' [50]

Glory shared: the glory of his Church (v. 22)

After praying for his immediate disciples, Jesus turns to pray for those who will subsequently come to faith in him—in other words, the Church through the ages. Another surprising statement follows, as Jesus says about these disciples, 'I have given them the glory that you gave me.' The glory he speaks of here is the glory of unity, and the kind of unity he means is a unity of organic intimacy, not structural rationalization. It is the sort of unity that Jesus himself enjoys with his Father—a unity of closeness and relationship, not of bureaucracy and organization. This unity is experienced whenever true believers meet with each other, even though they come from different countries, cultures and generations. Such unity is a gift from the ascended Lord who longs to replicate in their experience the bond he enjoys with his Father. It is in this way, Jesus says, that others will come to believe, because they too will want to experience such accepting and transforming grace.

Glory anticipated: the glory of his unveiling (v. 24)

The last reference to glory points forward to the even more distant future. Jesus prays that his disciples will one day be reunited with him so that they may 'see my glory'. The glory of his coming again and of the final unveiling of God's sovereign rule in the world, when all things will be reconciled to him, is what is in his mind. He is thinking of the time when his physical absence and his disciples' physical suffering will be over, when every knee will bow and every tongue confess that he, Jesus, is Christ the Lord 'to the glory of God the Father' (Philippians 2:10–11). We can anticipate it now. Indeed, this vision should be our daily expectation and inspiration. One day, however, we shall experience it. Only then will glory be fully revealed.

George Beasley-Murray rightly points out how remarkably similar this thought is to that of 1 John 3:2: 'Dear friends, now we are children of God, and what we will be has not yet been made known. But we know that when [Christ] appears, we shall be like him, for we shall see him as he is.'[51] The wonder is that when Christ's full glory is revealed, we will not only observe it but will also share in it ourselves. We too will be 'glorified' (Romans 8:30).

The glory of which Jesus speaks arches from an eternity past to an eternity future. It embraces both his disciples then and his disciples now. It encompasses his pre-incarnate existence, his life, death, resurrection, exaltation and his coming again. It is a glory conceived by love, the love between the Father and the Son; born by truth, the truth of God's word; mirrored in the holiness and unity of Jesus' disciples. It is a glory that will be seen one day in all its dazzling splendour as Jesus manifests his true identity to the world and completes the task that his work on earth began.

Questions

1. Which aspect of the glory of Christ mentioned here surprises you most, which aspect excites you most, and why?

2. How much do you think contemporary Christians look forward to 'the blessed hope—the glorious appearing of our great God and Saviour, Jesus Christ' (Titus 2:13). How much does the thought of Christ's return govern their motivations and actions?

24

The glory of the dying king

JOHN 18:1—19:37

The greatest paradox at the heart of the gospel is that the glory of Christ is most manifest in the shame of his death on the cross. In fact, that paradox *is* the heart of the gospel. Glory is normally associated with majesty, regal splendour, dazzling wealth and great dignity but, on the cross, Jesus redefines it. Stripped of power, rights, possessions, clothes and even of life itself, Jesus' glory shines with an unsurpassed radiance.

John presents Jesus throughout his trial and crucifixion as a king. The path he trod to Golgotha was not the road of a condemned criminal, but more, as one scholar has put it, like a royal progress tour.

He is an awesome king (18:1–24)

If you have ever attended an occasion involving royalty, you will have noticed several things about such events. First, they go according to plan, usually to a very exact timetable. The wishes of the royal participants are the only ones that count, and even the most hardened republican may find that they experience a sense of awe in the presence of majesty. When Jesus was arrested, tried and executed, he should have been the victim, with events taking place around him outside his control. But, as John tells us, nothing could be further from the truth.

When he is arrested in Gethsemane, Jesus is very much in command. He knows what is about to happen and steps forward to give himself up to his captors. They shrink back and fall to the ground, presumably at the awesomeness of his presence. He even takes charge, ordering them to release his disciples and then rebuking Peter for his well-meant but foolhardy attempt at defence. Jesus is the central figure, choreographing his own arrest.

John then recalls Jesus being taken to the house of Annas rather than straight to the high priest. In effect, John has anticipated the trial before Caiaphas, the high priest, in 11:50, so he doesn't record the details of that trial again here. Anyway, Annas, Caiaphas' father-in-law, was the real power behind the high priest's throne. He conducts a preliminary hearing of the charges against Jesus before sending him on to Caiaphas. The tone of this hearing is extraordinary, however: it turns out to be a classic courtroom debate in which Jesus refuses to admit wrong and in which Annas is unable to get the better of the prisoner.

In all that follows, Jesus continues to seem in command of the proceedings.

He is an alternative king (18:28 – 19:16)

Since the Jews had no power to exact the death penalty, they transmuted the charge of blasphemy into one of treason so that they might persuade Pilate, Rome's representative, to execute Jesus as a threat to the state. (Ironically, the Jewish leaders refuse to make themselves ceremonially unclean by entering Pilate's quarters, so that they will still be fit to eat the Passover meal. Little do they realize that their actions are about to lead to the sacrifice of *the* Passover lamb.)

In the trial that takes place before Pilate, there is a clash of two worlds, which leaves the Roman governor out of his depth, swimming in a mire of incomprehension.

Here are *two worlds of power*. Both talk about kingship, but they represent two worldviews even while using the same words. Jesus tells Pilate, frankly, that his 'kingdom is not of this world' (18:36). It does not, therefore, run on the lines that earthly kingdoms do, resorting to force, military might and the crushing of opposition by the imposition of power. It deals with wrong by absorbing it, by bearing away its consequences and by opening up the possibility of forgiveness and a new start. The way of the world provokes retaliation and further wrongdoing; the way of Jesus breaks the cycle of retaliation and shatters our desire to carry on doing wrong. Pilate thinks that power is on his side, but Jesus tells him plainly that the only power he has is the power that God, not Caesar, has granted to him (19:11).

Here also are *two worlds of truth*. From kingship, their discussion moves to the meaning of truth. Pilate asks, 'What is truth?', knowing that, for him, truth is whatever is politically expedient, whatever will please the Roman Caesar. Jesus has a very different definition of truth. He came to speak truth in a world riddled with lies, deception and half-truth. 'Everyone on the side of truth,' Jesus says, 'listens to me' (18:37). He is, in his own person, the measure of what is true.

He is a strong king (19:17)

The ritual of crucifixion was designed to reduce its victim to total weakness before stringing him up on a cross, exposed to public derision, and leaving him to die a lingering death. Jesus endured the ritual to the full. Flogged, possibly twice (once by way of investigation and later, more severely, after sentence), ridiculed as a king, subjected to a mock coronation and sentenced to death, he is then forced, in that weakened state, to carry his cross-beam through the streets of Jerusalem to the place of execution. But John recalls that Jesus was not cowed by all this and carried his own cross the full way to his execution. He remained a strong and sufficient king to the end. The torture and humiliation of the previous hours had left him undefeated, unbeaten, unbowed and unconquered.

He is a universal king (19:19–22)

It was the custom to pin a notice to the cross, announcing the crime for which the prisoner was being executed. In Jesus' case it read 'Jesus of Nazareth, the King of the Jews.' This sign, not unnaturally, provoked a complaint from the Jewish leaders, who asked for it to be made clear that Jesus had only claimed to be their king and was not, in their view, entitled to the name. Whether Pilate was being deliberately provocative or consciously ironic, we do not know, but the announcement of Jesus' kingship remained for all to see, turning his cross into a throne.

It is equally significant that the sign was written in three languages: Aramaic, the language of the locality; Latin, the language of government; and Greek, the language of culture. Here was a man who was dying as a king for all people—a universal Saviour—not a tribal ruler dying exclusively for one people or one nation. The embrace of his mercy and love is worldwide.

He is a compassionate king (19:25–27)

It is an extraordinary aspect of John's story that, even in the midst of extreme suffering, Jesus takes care of his mother's needs and makes provision for her. As the eldest son in the family, it would have been his responsibility to do so. He might have been forgiven if, on this occasion, other concerns took priority. In fact, however, he manages to commend Mary into the care of 'the disciple whom he loved'—possibly the writer of the Gospel himself. Jesus' action is totally consistent with what the other Gospels report concerning the way his compassion towards others continued right to the end. Luke, for example, adds other examples of his care: Jesus restores the severed ear of the high priest's servant (22:51), expresses concern for the weeping women of Jerusalem (23:28) and welcomes the dying thief into paradise (23:43).

We have grown so accustomed to the compassion of Jesus that we fail to register how astonishing it is. In contrast to the kings of the world, this king rules by serving and by giving himself to a degree well beyond anything that would be considered reasonable, however that might be measured. This is the meaning of grace, however.

He is a liberating king (19:28–37)

Two important details in John's account of the crucifixion, which can easily pass unnoticed, give us the clue to what he really believed was taking place that fateful day. In verse 29, he mentions that Jesus was offered a sponge filled with drink on 'a stalk of the hyssop plant'. Then, in verse 33, he reports that the soldiers 'did not break his legs' to hasten Jesus' death. Both of these verses echo details about the Passover lamb, which was offered as a means of setting Israel at liberty from Egypt (Exodus 12:21–23, 46), and both complement the clue already given in the account of Jesus' trial. John told us, in 19:14, that Jesus was condemned to death at the sixth hour on 'the day of Preparation of Passover Week'. That was the hour at which the slaughtering of lambs for the Passover began.

These clues drive us to the inevitable conclusion that Jesus is *the* Passover lamb. At last, we see 'the Lamb of God, who takes away the sin of the world' (John 1:29) fulfilling the purpose for which he came. His death is the means by which people of every era and nation can be set free from oppression and bondage. Crucifixion day is liberation day.

If we had planned to reveal the glory of Christ in the world, we would probably have chosen to do it by a display of majesty and power. The scene would have been strewn with light, colour, angels, choirs and musicians. God chose an altogether different path, and yet his glory was never brighter than when it shone from the throne of Calvary.

✣

Questions

1. 'Did e'er such love and sorrow meet, or thorns compose so rich a crown?' (Isaac Watts). Spend some time surveying 'the wondrous cross' and turn your thoughts into prayers of thanksgiving, devotion or anguish to God.

2. Read at least one other Gospel account of the crucifixion. If 'king' and 'Passover lamb' are the two key themes in John's Gospel, what dominant themes or Old Testament allusions do you find in the accounts of Matthew, Mark and Luke?

25

The glory of the risen Lord

JOHN 20:1–31

Most mornings I hear words like these over the breakfast table: 'So that's what it was. Of course! It's obvious!' They occur when the answer to yesterday's crossword is revealed in the newspaper. The trouble is that what is obvious today, with the answers in front of us, wasn't obvious the night before when we struggled unsuccessfully to work out the clues. So it is with the resurrection. Two thousand years later, we know that Easter Sunday followed Good Friday, so we read about Jesus' crucifixion in the light of the resurrection and wonder why the disciples didn't get it. But for them, the crucifixion spelt a puzzling and disappointing end to the hopes they had placed in Jesus. It didn't make sense. The clues about what would happen next remained a mystery—until, that is, they encountered the risen Lord.

John 20 is more than just the next chapter of the book. It is the place where the last piece of the jigsaw falls into place and makes sense of all that has gone before. It picks up a lot of the clues that have been scattered throughout the Gospel and decodes them. We only have room here to mention a few that display the glory of Jesus in a new light.

The glory of creation renewed (v. 1)

The account of the resurrection begins with the phrase 'Early on the first day of the week'. It looks a straightforward enough statement, but it isn't quite as innocent as it seems. The other Gospels consistently speak of the resurrection as happening 'on the third day'. Why does John use different terminology? It's because John wants to say that something new commenced on the day when Jesus rose from the dead. Tom Wright points out that Jesus was condemned on the sixth day of the week, rested in the tomb on the seventh and rose early on the eighth to mark the beginning of a new creation.[52]

This Gospel has always shown an interest in creation. In John 1 we read that the Word brought creation into existence. In John 5:17 we read that he continues to sustain it. Jesus worked miracles in the arena of creation. His concern to restore peace, health, sight and even life shows that creation matters. True Christianity is not about escaping this world to a higher and more important spiritual world, but about God renewing the present creation. The resurrection signals that this renewal of creation has begun. This world, for so long out of harmony with God and consequently out of sorts with itself, is now being remade and its brokenness healed. Through the resurrection, Jesus, the life-giver, gives new life not just to a few representative human beings but to all his fallen creation.

The glory of light restored (v. 1)

Next, John mentions, significantly if briefly, that Mary went to the tomb 'while it was still dark'. The metaphors of darkness and light have threaded their way through the Gospel. Darkness symbolized those whose lives were riddled with evil. It is used even more to symbolize the cross that Jesus was to endure (9:4; 12:35; 13:30). In contrast, Jesus is seen to be 'the light of the world' (8:12; 9:5) who shines in the darkness (1:5) and sets people free to walk in the light (8:12; 12:46).

Here, darkness makes its appearance for the last time. With the resurrection, the darkness of the world is being dispelled. The tomb is empty. The Lord is risen. Evil is defeated. Death is vanquished.

The light, which people had constantly tried to snuff out, is shining irrepressibly once more.

The glory of sight rewarded (vv. 3–9)

Peter and 'the other disciple' are summoned to the empty tomb. While Peter, true to character, impetuously enters the tomb, the other disciple hangs back. When he does enter, we are told that 'he saw and believed'. We learned earlier that seeing miracles does not automatically lead to belief (6:26; 12:37). There is a seeing that goes deeper, however, a perceiving of God at work—which leads to faith. Seeing does not necessarily cheapen faith, but may prove to be its handmaid. That is how it is for 'the other disciple', who sees with his physical eyes the greatest sight of all—the tomb is empty, the dead body no longer there—and perceives with his spiritual eyes the significance of what has happened. In spite of not having a perfect understanding, he responds in the only reasonable way possible—by believing.

The same issue will surface again when Jesus speaks with Thomas: 'Because you have seen me, you have believed; blessed are those who have not seen and yet have believed' (v. 29). Seeing the evidence with physical eyes was good. Not seeing, yet still believing, is even better.

The glory of truth recognized (vv. 11–18)

Mary's encounter with the risen Jesus is one of the most touching and most human episodes in the whole story. Full of painful grief, she fails at first to recognize Jesus through her tears, mistaking him for the gardener. But the speaking of her name is enough. The good shepherd, who 'calls his own sheep by name' (10:3), has laid down his life and has now taken it up again. As sheep recognize the shepherd's voice, so Mary immediately recognizes the voice of Jesus.

The identity of Jesus is one of the mysteries that thread their way through John's Gospel. The opening chapter warned us that Jesus was not recognized by his own people and hinted that their failure to do so was caused by unbelief. Again and again, Jesus appeared to be a puzzling figure, who conducted himself in mysterious ways and spoke in riddles. People argued about who he was. Now the truth is out, and Mary recognizes who he really is. She calls him 'Teacher', which may be no more than a respectful term for a rabbi, but she hears him speak of returning to his Father and his God and so she confidently tells the disciples, 'I have seen the Lord!' 'Lord' had been one of their favourite ways of addressing Jesus, but here it is invested with a new meaning. At last the truth is emerging: Jesus is being seen as the Messiah.

The glory of the Spirit released (vv. 19–23)

When Jesus later appears to ten of his disciples (still cowering behind locked doors, presumably afraid that the authorities will want to interrogate them about the missing body), he greets them and convinces them that he is alive again by showing them his wounds. The real purpose of his appearance, though, is to impart the Holy Spirit to them. Here is an anticipation of the Day of Pentecost, a foretaste of what they and others will experience a few weeks later as they gather together once more.

Jesus had taught his disciples that when he left the earth, his Spirit would come to them. Now, as the time for his departure gets close, he personally introduces his Spirit to his disciples and so builds the bridge from one stage of the salvation story to the next. The time for revealing God's glory through the physical life of one man is past. The time for revealing God's glory through the universal ministry of his Spirit has come.

The glory of unbelief reversed (vv. 24–31)

The climax of the initial resurrection appearances comes when Jesus appears again to his disciples a week later, when Thomas is present. It would be good to know why Thomas was so unbelieving about the claim that his friends had made that Jesus was alive again. I suppose resurrections don't happen every day! But was he naturally disposed to being cynical? Was he still suffering from confusing and jumbled emotions? Or, given his absence first time around, was he just a natural loner who never went along with the crowd? Doubt of the kind that Thomas exhibits may be a genuine struggle to find the truth, in which case the questions should not be suppressed but honestly confronted. Some doubt, however, masks an unwillingness to submit to truth and is of the kind mentioned earlier by John when he warned that persistent unbelief is the very essence of sin (16:9).

Having been invited to examine the physical wounds of Jesus, Thomas confesses his faith with the words, 'My Lord and my God!' In the incarnation, the Word became flesh. Here at the resurrection, the human Jesus stands before Thomas in his battered flesh and is declared to be divine—the Word, one with the Father. Human sight and human touch are called into play to confirm the truth that faith dared to believe. It was a staggering claim. The Roman emperor liked to be hailed as 'Lord and God'. But, in the resurrection, Jesus asserts his right to rule in his world and to be its sole and divine sovereign—an assertion that was to prove profoundly unsettling to any who thought of themselves as being in control.

We may not have had the opportunity of seeing the risen Christ with our physical eyes, but we can see the glory of the risen Lord with the eyes of faith. We know that our faith is based both on the eyewitness evidence of his first disciples and on his Spirit's continuing activity in bringing glory to Jesus around the world. With Thomas, we have good reason to affirm that Jesus is Lord and God.

✤

Questions

1. To what extent does it matter to you whether or not Jesus literally rose from the dead? What hinges on it? See 1 Corinthians 15:12–19.

2. How does this chapter help you talk to those who might be doubtful about who Jesus is?

26

The glory of the hope restorer

JOHN 21:1–25

The last chapter of John's Gospel is a bonus chapter. The end of chapter 20 sounds like a final fanfare and would have been sufficient to bring the Gospel to a suitable conclusion. But just when you think you've heard the closing notes played, the music starts again and another refrain is performed. It gives us one last glimpse of the glory of Jesus—a very personal one that revolves mostly around the figure of Peter. It is written with such attention to detail—'reality effects', they've been called—that it reads like an eyewitness account that has been treasured in memory over the years.

While Peter plays an important part, though, it is actually Jesus who takes the leading role.

Hope for fishermen who failed to catch fish (vv. 1–14)

Back in Galilee, spurred on by Peter, some of the disciples decide to go fishing. This decision has often been judged quite harshly. One commentator calls it 'aimless activity undertaken in desperation'. Another says that it shows how Peter was in a state of denial about his betrayal of Christ and so chose to revert to his old life. But John certainly doesn't attribute such base motives to the disciples. The other Gospels tell us that Jesus had instructed them to return to Galilee and wait for him there. When they did so, it would have been the most natural thing for them, as men who had been fishing all their lives, to get out their boats to pass their time. They were unlikely to resist the lure of the lake.

But the disciples seem to have lost their touch, because, even though the hours of darkness were the best time to fish, 'that night they caught nothing'. They were total failures. Then Jesus steps in. With *commanding authority* he tells them to throw the net on the other side of the boat and they will catch a huge number of fish. What was it, I wonder, about the way he said this that made them obey? Hardened fishermen don't usually take advice from others, especially if they're weary and frustrated, having just worked a long shift. They hadn't yet recognized the one who was shouting to them from the shore, but there must have been something about him that made them listen and obey. What an irony that a carpenter proved better than experienced fishermen at their craft! But then, this carpenter is the one who made the world.

The incident testifies to the continuing *magnetic attraction* of Jesus. No sooner has the miracle happened than Peter recognizes that it is Jesus who has shouted to them, and he decides to dive into the water to go and greet him. A curious detail is added to tell us that Peter put on his outer garment before jumping into the water. This seems a strange action. It might have been more sensible to leave the garment behind rather than get it wet! But some suggest that it reveals Peter's state of mind. Like Adam and Eve covering themselves up in shame before God in Eden, so Peter is still so ashamed of his denial of Jesus that he must, in some measure, hide from him while at the same time being irresistibly attracted to him. Then again, perhaps it's no more than a typically impetuous action on Peter's part—the sort we have come to expect.

The commanding authority of Jesus is matched by his *abundant provision*. Once the disciples obey Jesus, the trawl of fish they harvest is massive: 153 large ones. Explanations are rife as to why this figure is mentioned. The most obvious answer is that this is the number of fish in the net, and the catch was so impressive that someone bothered to count them. Most other explanations are less obvious. Some believe that it was the number of known species of fish and so symbolizes the way in which Jesus' disciples would, from then on, 'catch' people from every nation on the earth. This may be so, but John's Gospel doesn't speak about the disciples as 'fishers of men'. Perhaps it is a sign that the promised abundance of the new age, which the Messiah would bring, has commenced (see Ezekiel 47).

Hope for a disciple who failed to stand firm (vv. 15–19)

Breakfast prepared, it's time for Jesus to do business with Peter. The time (early in the morning), the place (a charcoal fire) and the questioning (three times) ensure that we see this conversation as an undoing of Peter's denial of Christ. Here indeed is abundant grace.

We should note that *failure is confronted*. Jesus does not carry on as if no denial had taken place. To do so would have left Peter with deep uncertainties and regrets that would have dogged any subsequent ministry. When failure is confronted and repentance exercised, then *forgiveness is bestowed*. Peter's love for Jesus is expressed three times—once for each occasion that it was previously denied. Nothing is to be made of the different words for 'love' that are found in the original Greek, in contrast to the speculations of some commentators. They are simply variations on a theme. Each time Peter confesses his love, his *mission is restored*. Over and above the abundance of Jesus' common grace, seen in his provision of so many fish, we now witness the abundance of his special grace as he recommissions Peter as the shepherd of his sheep. The shepherding imagery reminds us of Jesus' teaching about the good shepherd. As Mark Stibbe points out, it means that 'Jesus is seen helping Peter confront the fact that he behaved like a hired hand (who runs away in the hour of danger), and (is) calling him back to his vocation as a model shepherd.'[53]

There is more. The commission renewed here is not one that will make Peter a celebrity, nor does it assure him that his ministry will be one of unalloyed success and special protection. It will be a mission that demands the ultimate cost, because *martyrdom is predicted*. The promise that, in his old age, he will stretch out his hands and be led where he does not want to go is a colloquial way of talking about crucifixion—the fate he would share with his Master. But it would also be the means by which, like his Master, he 'would glorify God'. Beyond any miracles or preaching, it was to be in Peter's dying that God would be honoured most. God does not work one way through Jesus and a different way through his Church. He still brings a fallen world to himself as his disciples live in weakness, endure suffering and die to self. If we want the glory of Jesus to be seen in the world, this is how we must continue to display it.

Hope for a world that failed to take heed (vv. 20–23)

Trying to deflect the attention from himself, Peter asks Jesus about 'the disciple whom Jesus loved'. We cannot be sure who this disciple was. He may well have been the author of the Gospel; hence many think of him as John. We must be careful, though, not to fall into the same trap as Peter and indulge in useless speculation at the expense of focusing on our obedience to Jesus' calling on our own lives.

Peter's question leads Jesus to speak of the future and to assert again that the day will come when he will return. Jesus' enemies had sought to get rid of him and thought they had done so on the cross. The resurrection had proved them incapable of achieving their end. Nor would the world rid itself of him when he ascended to his Father. That would only signal a temporary departure, and one day Jesus will come back, when he will be recognized by all and reign over all. Then, he will complete the work he has begun of rescuing the world and reconciling all to his Father. Then, his glory will no longer be veiled, but manifest in all its undisguised brilliance.

Jesus brings hope to fishermen who had failed to catch fish, to a disciple who had failed to stand firm and to a world that had failed to live in harmony with its Creator. In each case, he gives us a further glimpse of his glory. This final reprise arranges the music of glory in fresh ways. It captures the glory of Jesus' abundant provision in the face of our emptiness, the glory of his amazing grace in the face of our failure and the glory of his assured return in the face of our despair.

From first to last, John's Gospel speaks of the glory of Jesus. His glory, truth to tell, was sometimes veiled, yet on other occasions it was majestically revealed to those who had the eyes to see. Those who have the eyes of faith continue to see the glory of Christ and offer him their adoration and obedience as a result. They seek, too, to enhance his glory, as Peter was to do, by walking in his footsteps. This glory is one that the world has yet to see in all its unconcealed splendour. But one day, when he returns, the glory of the One and Only who came from the Father will be visible to all.

Questions

1. Think back over John's Gospel. How has it helped you to see the glory of Jesus more fully? Would you say that the portrait painted here is of a figure who was 'full of grace and truth'?

2. If Jesus were to ask you the question he asked Peter—'Do you love me?'—how would you reply? Would he need to drag an embarrassed answer out of you or would you give him your willing affirmation? What might your answer mean in terms of your following Jesus?

For further reading

D.A. Carson, *The Gospel According to John*, Pillar Commentary, Eerdmans & IVP, 1991.

Andreas Kostenberger, *Encountering John*, Baker Academic, 2002.

Bruce Milne, *The Message of John*, The Bible Speaks Today, IVP, 1993.

Tom Wright, *John for Everyone* (2 vols), SPCK, 2002.

Notes

1   H.D. McDonald, *Jesus: Human and Divine*, Pickering & Inglis, 1968, p. 140.
2   Quoted in Philip Yancey, *The Jesus I Never Knew*, Marshall Pickering, 1995, p. 34.
3   Bruce Milne, *The Message of John* (Bible Speaks Today), IVP, 1993, p. 46.
4   Milne, *The Message of John*, p. 36.
5   John Goldingay, 'Your iniquities have made a separation between you and your God' in John Goldingay (ed.), *Atonement Today*, SPCK, 1995, p. 39.
6   D.A. Carson, *The Gospel According to John* (Pillar Commentary Series), Eerdmans and IVP, 1991, p. 171.
7   William Barclay, *The Gospel of John*, Vol. 1 (Daily Study Bible), St Andrew Press, 1955, p. 87.
8   Yancey, *The Jesus I Never Knew*, p. 21.
9   C.H. Dodd, *The Founder of Christianity*, Collins, 1971, p. 147.
10 *The Daily Telegraph*, 10 April 1982.
11 Quoted in John Stott, *Basic Christianity*, IVP, 1958, pp. 104ff.
12 Tom Wright, *John for Everyone*, Part 1, SPCK, 2002, p. 30.
13 *The Times*, 2 November 2001. The story was frequently told and occurred again in the *Education Guardian* on 19 August 2002 as a warning to students about the effects of alcohol.
14 C.S. Lewis, *Mere Christianity*, 50th anniversary edition, HarperCollins, 2002, p. 121.
15 John Stott, *The Bible: Book for Today*, IVP, 1982, p. 20.
16 Robert Putnam, *Bowling Alone: The Collapse and Revival of American Community*, Simon & Schuster, 2000.
17 Anne Graham Lotz, *Just Give Me Jesus*, Word, 2000, pp. 95f.
18 Ben Witherington III, *John's Wisdom: A Commentary on the Fourth Gospel*, Lutterworth Press, 1995, p. 95.

19 John White, *The Fight: A Practical Handbook of Christian Living*, IVP, 1977, p. 101.

20 Carson, *John*, p. 243.

21 William Temple, *Readings in St John's Gospel*, Macmillan, 1968, p.105.

22 Tom Wright, *John for Everyone*, Part I, SPCK, 2002, p. 62.

23 See Andrew Lincoln, *Truth on Trial: The Lawsuit Motif in the Fourth Gospel*, Hendrickson, 2000.

24 A.M. Ramsey, *The Glory of God and the Transfiguration of Christ*, Longmans, Green & Co, 1949, p. 65.

25 John Calvin, *The Gospel According to St John 1—10*, trans. T.H.L. Parker, St Andrew Press, 1959, p. 145.

26 J.B. Lightfoot, *St John's Gospel: A Commentary*, OUP, 1956, p. 160.

27 Calvin, *John 1—10*, p. 153.

28 William Barclay, *The Gospel of Matthew*, Vol 2 (Daily Study Bible), St Andrew Press, 1958, p. 117.

29 Augustine, 'Homilies on the Gospel of John, Tractate 25', *Nicene and Post-Nicene Fathers*, Series I, Vol. VII, T&T Clark and Eerdmans, n.d.

30 George R. Beasley-Murray, *Preaching the Gospel from the Gospels*, Hendrickson, 1996, pp. 95ff.

31 Temple, *Readings*, p. 149.

32 Barclay, *John*, Vol 2, p. 46.

33 Alastair Campbell, *Rediscovering Pastoral Care*, Darton, Longman & Todd, 1981, p. 47.

34 John Calvin, *The Gospel According to St John 11—21 and the First Epistle of John*, trans. T.H.L. Parker, St Andrew Press, 1961, p. 13.

35 Milne, *John*, p. 166.

36 Milne, *John*, p. 162.

37 Tom Wright, *Mark for Everyone*, SPCK, 2001, pp. 146ff.

38 Ramsey, *Glory*, p. 67.

39 Carson, *John*, p. 462.

40 John Stott, *Christ the Liberator*, Hodder & Stoughton, 1971, p. 16.

41 Donald Kraybill, *The Upside-Down Kingdom*, Herald Press, 1978, p. 293.

42 T.W. Manson, *The Church's Ministry*, Hodder & Stoughton, 1948, p. 27.

43 J.B. Philips' translation of John 14:6 in *The New Testament in Modern English* (first published 1960).

44 Dorothy L. Sayers, 'The Other Six Deadly Sins', an address given at the Caxton Hall, 23 October 1941.

45 Thomas à Kempis, *The Imitation of Christ* (many editions), book 3, ch. 56.

46 David Gooding, *In the School of Christ: A Study of Christ's Teaching on Holiness. John 13—17*, Gospel Folio Press, 1995, p. 137.

47 Milne, *John*, pp. 219ff.

48 John Stott, *The Message of Romans* (Bible Speaks Today), IVP, 1994, p. 53.

49 Thomas A. Smail, *Reflected Glory: The Spirit in Christ and Christians*, Hodder & Stoughton, 1975, pp. 11, 12.

50 Carson, *John*, p. 561.

51 Beasley-Murray, *John*, p. 304.

52 Tom Wright, *John for Everyone*, Part 2, SPCK, 2002, p. 140.

53 Mark W.G. Stibbe, *John*, Sheffield Academic Press, 1993, p. 213.

A Fruitful Life

Abiding in Christ as seen in John 15

Tony Horsfall

'It is my desire through these pages to point you back to the simplicity of a life lived out of relationship with Jesus Christ. A life of intimacy, of abiding in him, is the source and spring of all other activity and endeavour. The branch bears fruit because it abides in the vine.'

In *A Fruitful Life* we ponder the teaching of Jesus in John 15, the famous 'vine' passage. He is preparing his disciples for his departure and describing how they can be effective witnesses in a hostile world. Just as his instructions revolutionized their lives, so a proper understanding of what he is saying can revolutionize our lives also. It is the heart of the gospel message: the only way to live the Christian life is to allow Jesus to live his life in us and through us.

This book includes material for individual reflection and also questions for group discussion.

ISBN 1 84101 335 8   £6.99
Available from your local Christian bookshop or, in case of difficulty, direct from BRF using the order form on page 159.

God on the Inside

The Holy Spirit in Holy Scripture

Nigel G. Wright

What does it mean to 'know' God? Far more than intellectual knowledge, to 'know' God is to engage in a personal relationship, to sense God's active presence in our lives on a daily basis—and that's where the work of the Holy Spirit comes in. The first Christians knew it was by the Spirit that they first believed and experienced God's love poured into their hearts. Since then, the third person of the Trinity has often been overlooked, even neglected.

In the last 30 years, however, there has been an explosion of interest in the Spirit. Christians around the world have realized how all experience is touched in some way by the Spirit's gracious activity. This book examines from the Bible why the Holy Spirit is far more important than most of us realize. It goes on to show that we need to take a fresh look at who the Spirit is and what the Spirit does—God on the inside of those who believe, on the inside of creation itself as Lord and Giver of life and, indeed, on the inside of God's own being.

ISBN 1 84101 484 2   £7.99
Available from your local Christian bookshop or, in case of difficulty, direct from BRF using the order form on page 159.

PBC John

A Bible commentary for every day

Richard A. Burridge

John's Gospel is often given to people as a readable account of Jesus of Nazareth, yet it is also a sublime masterpiece that has occupied theologians and mystics for centuries. It has been described as 'a book in which a child may paddle but an elephant can swim deep'. At the same time, however, it is still a story—the story of Jesus' deeds and words, his signs and teaching, and how these led to his arrest, death and resurrection.

By following the flow of John's narrative, and showing how it is patterned and devised, this commentary unpacks the text to help the reader grow in understanding and faith.

The People's Bible Commentary covers the whole Bible, with a daily reading approach that brings together both personal devotion and reflective study. Combining the latest scholarship with straightforward language and a reverent attitude to scripture, it aims to instruct the head and warm the heart.

ISBN 1 84101 029 4   £8.99
Available from your local Christian bookshop or, in case of difficulty, direct from BRF using the order form on page 159.

ORDER FORM

REF	TITLE	PRICE	QTY	TOTAL
335 0	*A Fruitful Life*	£6.99		
484 5	*God on the Inside*	£7.99		
029 4	*PBC John*	£8.99		

POSTAGE AND PACKING CHARGES					Postage and packing:	
Order value	UK	Europe	Surface	Air Mail	Donation:	
£7.00 & under	£1.25	£3.00	£3.50	£5.50	**Total enclosed:**	
£7.01–£30.00	£2.25	£5.50	£6.50	£10.00		
Over £30.00	free	prices on request				

Name _____ Account Number _____

Address _____

_____ Postcode _____

Telephone Number _____ Email _____

Payment by: ❏ Cheque ❏ Mastercard ❏ Visa ❏ Postal Order ❏ Maestro

Card no. ❏❏❏❏ ❏❏❏❏ ❏❏❏❏ ❏❏❏❏

Expires ❏❏ ❏❏ Security code ❏❏❏ Issue no. ❏❏❏

Signature _____ Date _____

All orders must be accompanied by the appropriate payment.

Please send your completed order form to:
BRF, First Floor, Elsfield Hall, 15–17 Elsfield Way, Oxford OX2 8FG
Tel. 01865 319700 / Fax. 01865 319701 Email: enquiries@brf.org.uk

❏ Please send me further information about BRF publications.

Available from your local Christian bookshop.   BRF is a Registered Charity

brf

Resourcing your spiritual journey

through...

- Bible reading notes
- Books for Advent & Lent
- Books for Bible study and prayer
- Books to resource those working with under 11s in school, church and at home

- Quiet days and retreats
- Training for primary teachers and children's leaders
- Godly Play
- Barnabas RE Days

For more information, visit the **brf** website at **www.brf.org.uk**